Getting
INSIDE
Your MAN

Also by Leroy Scott

Unbreaking the Heart

Love Notes

Creating Possibilities in Marriage

Getting INSIDE Your MAN

A Woman's Guide to Understanding the Man She Loves

LEROY SCOTT

Copyright © 2013 by Leroy Scott

All rights reserved. No part of this book may be reproduced or transmitted in any form or by any means, electronic or mechanical, including photocopying, recording, or any information storage and retrieval system, without permission in writing from Leroy Scott.

ISBN: 978-0-9895344-4-4

Printed in the United States of America

Examples cited in this book are composites of the author's actual cases. Names and facts have been changed and rearranged to maintain confidentiality.

Except as noted, scripture quotations are from NEW AMERICAN STANDARD BIBLE®, Copyright © 1960, 1962, 1963, 1968, 1971, 1972, 1973, 1975, 1977, 1995 by The Lockman Foundation. Used by permission. Bible Gateway (www.biblegateway.com) is the resource used for downloading the quotations.

∞ This paper meets the requirements of ANSI/NISO Z39.48-1992 (Permanence of Paper)

This book is dedicated to every woman who loves a man; who nurtures a son to responsible manhood; who gives all the love she has and all too often gets nothing back but heartbreak. May this book give you hope and the insight into men you need to change your life forever!

Contents

Preface ix
Introduction: The Manhood Crisis xvii
1: A Man's Ultimate Life Question 1
2: How Men and Women Think 7
3: How Men Measure Manhood 19
4: Inside a Man's World 29
5: His Sexuality and Sexual Struggle 39
6: The Role of Mom and Dad 47
7: The Importance of Being a Son 57
8: A Man's Fear and Anger 71
9: Principles, Priorities and Power 81
10: The Power of Perspective 95
11: When Men Fail 105
12: Moving Him From Logic to Locomotion 113
13: Long Roads and Dead Ends 127
14: Funnel Living 135
15: Saving Our Sons 141
16: Celebrating Manhood 151

Afterword	157
Index	159
About the Author	169
Contact Information & Other Products	170

TO THE GIRLS AND WOMEN OF THIS GENERATION

The first intention of this book is to help women understand men and explain why men act the way they do. I hope as a result you will gain insight into how you can better position yourself to have a healthy and long-term relationship with a man. It has been my observation that women want a life companion who is truly a *Godly man*—that is, a man who loves God, his wife, his children and his community and, in loving them, takes responsibility for caring for them and ensuring that his impact and influence is reflective of what God ultimately desires for them all.

The insights to be gained from reading this book do not suggest that a woman can change a man, but there are some things you can do to get the results you desire in your relationship. It's not that men don't know what it means to be a Godly man, but they have moved away from the true essence of manhood. Hopefully this book will encourage you and help you to encourage and support him.

The second intention of this book is to help women (and men) to raise happy, healthy sons who will grow into the men all women seek as soul mates. Here you will learn the different roles mothers and fathers play in this process and how you, as a mother, can raise a wonderful son even if his father is not actively involved in the boy's life.

There are some basic necessities of life that men need in the context of relationships beyond food, water, shelter and sex. Things like respect, companionship and sexual neediness seem to be basic necessities for a man. The goal for a woman is to ensure that she taps into these needs to unlock his full potential. That's right, I said it: women have the power to unlock a man's full potential. God designed you that way. Men can certainly get by on their own, but it is not good for them to be alone because the potential God put in them has to be unlocked and *they don't have the key!*

Yes, you women hold the key to bringing out the best in a man. I always wondered what Adam would have become without Eve; what life would have been like for him alone. God knew exactly what he was doing when he gave Eve to Adam. She didn't complete him, she complemented him. Everything about her was exactly fitted for him, like a piece to a puzzle. So, ladies, complementing your man is the key to completing the puzzle. You are made to complement him physically *and* you will actually strengthen and encourage him when you *compliment* him verbally. You are made to cheer for him, to push him over the goal line, to get him in the end zone. It draws a man's heart closer to a woman, and if you really love him, you will do that happily. Remember, if he doesn't win, you lose. If you feel like you can win alone, on your own, and you convey that message to your man, you will cause him to lose for you.

Men are primarily influenced from the outside—his parents, the people he admires and hugely by the media. But I am trying to take you to his inside and the things about him that are not so obvious. God works deep inside a man to make sure that you become the essence of his soul's desire. God puts love in him for you. Your man knows what his responsibility to God is regarding you, but it is your job to pull it out of him—to transform him from the inside out.

Men need to be touched, encouraged, given neck massages and back rubs—anything that shows them you appreciate them. A woman who was never taught to celebrate a man is a woman who will really struggle in any intimate relationship.

This book helps you to focus on the things that matter. For example, respect. Respect is big for a man. For men, respect is more important than love. As a matter of fact, when you respect a man, he actually feels you love him. And it's not just you saying you respect him or not disrespecting him in public by calling him names or demeaning his character. It's more about you appreciating him. When you appreciate your man, you reinforce how much you respect him. When you don't appreciate him, he feels you don't respect him. So create an environment of appreciation and celebration of the man he is. Sometimes a simple head rub or back rub does it. Sometimes you have to tell it to him. And other times it's just looking at him in a way that shows you appreciate him. For men, it is truly better to give than it is to receive. Men love to give to the people they love. They adore making sure you have the things you need. But more than giving you the things you need, they love seeing your response. The response you give to what they give you is more valuable to them than the gift itself.

Men are more acclimated to loyalty than they are to love. I was trying to assist a guy, who lately became a very good friend of mine, as he struggled in his relationship by helping him to understand love. He couldn't really grasp the concept of love. Coming from his background and the ideology of gangs, hard men, and imprisoned men, he understood loyalty as a critical part of how they build relationships. But love is about patience, kindness, gentleness, giving unconditionally and treating others the way you want to be treated. Loyalty has to do with commitment, bargaining, dedication and indebtedness. Men understand these principles better than they do the principles associated with love. They understand the concept of "you owe me one" and "don't rat out your friends." They live and breathe these principles. But love is sometimes very difficult for them to get to. Men have challenges with issues of the heart (something I go into in greater depth in *Unbreaking the Heart* [Leroy Scott Ministries, 2010]). Women mistakenly perceive this as a negative thing but, in essence, it is a very good thing because, when a man starts with loyalty and his woman understands that, they can easily transition to love.

Deep inside every man is an intrinsic desire to be good. The problem is that most often he is not good and he lives in a culture that looks down on men because women have claimed that they are just simply no good. Parents warn their daughters about a man just wanting one thing and far too many men have made babies that they didn't take care of. So good is far from the reality for men. They actually feel like they are behind the eight ball on this one. They feel that they have to prove themselves. To counter this and build your man up, as a woman you must constantly focus on what is good about him and encourage him in being good—especially if you really have a good man. If you tear him down, make him feel nasty or dirty he will withdraw from you and eventually consider that you really don't love him.

Men also need to know that you desire them sexually. For men, sex doesn't begin in the bedroom. It begins in the head. Stimulation begins in the brain with the words you speak to him, the things you say to him and the way you make him feel inside. His ears are more in tune with you than anything. A

Preface: To the Girls and Women of This Generation

woman can plant feelings in a man that grow to be very positive thoughts about her. When she does this, he is increasingly sexually attracted to her. He also wants to hear you say great things about him. He hates it when you always talk to him about other people and never talk about him to him. It is more important for him to actually hear you say what you tell other people about him than it is for him to know you speak well about him.

Yes, men are sexual beings with high sex drives, but God made them that way and the deeper they fall in love with the woman God gives them, the more that woman will have to understand how to unlock his full potential. He is complete and what he needs is to be so well complimented that he is pulled to what God has called him to be and his wife can bask in the blessings God put in him for her.

After reading this book you will have gained insights and tools that will help take your relationship with your man to the next level. Everything you dreamed of, everything you ever wanted in your relationship, everything your parents and friends didn't know enough to tell you, I do know, I tell you and then I explain how to go about making your dreams come true.

The things I write about in this book are not just intellectual issues for me, they come from deep within. I have an intimate knowledge of the things I speak about: my own father was an absentee dad, and I have a long history of women in my family who were abused by men. My grandmother was murdered by a man in the name of love. So as I write to women about men, my aim is to help them to get inside the men in their lives, digging deep to discover and delight in their core being, thus totally enhancing their relationships. I want women to discover how to get the best out of their guys in every way so they never have to suffer as my grandmother did—or anything close to that. My ultimate objective is to see every woman win in what she wants the most—a good man.

I need to add a brief forewarning before you read further. Throughout this book you may think that I am making some sweeping generalizations: that all men are deadbeat dads or, even at their best, would never be candidates for Father of the Year; that all women are too soft, or too emasculating, or have no idea how to treat a man; that all boys are victims of dysfunctional families and are doomed to follow in their (missing) fathers' footsteps or worse. Believe me, it is not my intention to make such broad assumptions or, worse, to be offensive to anyone. But in order to make my point, I needed to take the liberty of simplifying the situation we as a society find ourselves in today. I think no one will deny that we have a crisis on our hands—the crisis that has created an environment of crime, illicit sex, drugs and death on the streets.

Just a glance at the statistical research I cite in the Introduction should convince anyone. But let me be perfectly clear that it is not my intent to lump all men or women into any category. However, I do want you, the reader, to be impacted by the extent of the problem. I want to get as close to the truth as possible. So I tell it like it is, and sometimes the truth hurts. Yet, I don't want you to fall into deep despair or disconnection. I want to be real, relevant and relational, which is what I think not only you, the reader, but also I, myself, can appreciate.

I know there are whole, happy and healthy families out there. There are fathers and mothers who are wonderful examples for the rest of us (and I hope you are one of them). And, lest you think I believe all women should just stay home, clean the house and raise babies—not quite!

Preface: To the Girls and Women of This Generation

I think every woman has every right to work and tackle the world in ways that they were previously restricted from doing. However, I don't think they should *have* to. I do believe that is the role of the man. Not because she can't, but rather because she doesn't have to. I want to get that point across without offending the advancement of women over the decades.[1]

I believe a husband and wife should be equal partners in their marriage. I only wish that women can give up having to be men so that they can be women; not give up empowerment, but rather gain true empowerment by being able to rely on an accountable, responsible and faithful man.

Every woman deserves a great man in her life. And every woman deserves to have a *choice* whether to be a stay-at-home mom or follow a career that pleases her. I don't necessarily see barefoot, babies and apron strings as a disgrace to a woman if she has a man who takes care of her and his family. Women don't need Gucci shoes and power suits and BMWs and to be successful and accomplished. As a matter of fact many of my female clients who are successful professionals say they lack one thing in their lives and that's the thing they want more than any other. I am writing from the perspective of helping a woman get inside her man, to discover how to get the best out of him in every way. My ultimate objective is to see her win what she wants the most—a good man!

I believe it is a man's responsibility to provide for his family. I believe that is God's original intent for men. That should not be put on the shoulders of women. Children should not have to be in daycare at six months old—they should be with their mother. But, I'll stop before I get frustrated! My intention is to

---

[1] I often say that I would love to see my daughter graduate and go to medical school to study psychiatry and then marry a man who takes care of her while she

inspire men again; to motivate them—and encourage and give insight to women so they can help to call men forward.

Please share this book with your man and get his perspective, because there are many things in this book that will encourage him as well. Some of the things I've written about, men are not even aware of. When men read the book, they can gain affirming insights that will help them understand themselves better. I hope they will have "a-ha" moments and feel like someone has finally explained what they have always been trying to get people to understand about them. When this happens, men are inspired to "man up" and be all that God created them to be in their relationships.

Enjoy.

Leroy Scott

Leroy Scott MS, MDiv, NCC, LPC-LA, LMHC-FL

---

takes care of her home and never has to practice—at least not a rigorous 40 hours a week as a sole provider and breadwinner.

Introduction

THE MANHOOD CRISIS

Joe's Story

It was June 2008 and I was ending my day with what would be my final counseling session for the evening: an Employee Assistance referral from a major corporate company of a young African-American man who was having difficulty in his marriage. I'll call him "Joe." At 4:05 p.m. we began talking about how he and his wife were struggling with their communication and how Joe had been having financial challenges due to his mortgage rate being raised to a level he could no longer afford. By 4:30 p.m. we were discussing the loss of his mother when he was 13 and the poor relationship he had with his father, along with mention of mentors who had some level of influence on his life. Interestingly, the impact of not having a relationship with his father was making life just as difficult as the marriage challenges he was having. At 4:45 p.m. Joe's tears were more than he could handle; his pain was closer to the surface than he had realized. Despite all of his losses and his current challenges, however, Joe was still able to maintain a good front and have great success in many areas.

Then 4:50 p.m. came and Joe made an amazing proclamation. Most men would not have had the courage to say what Joe said, although deep inside they might feel it. He mumbled the words,

"Sometimes I feel like I'm not man enough." This statement would eventually give him permission to explore the possibility that he might not be "man enough" or, even if he were, how would he know unless he had examined the idea?

Joe didn't pose the question of his manhood because he wasn't working, or wasn't married—or even because he wasn't happy. He was literally tapping into one of the deepest and darkest corners of manhood and acknowledging that, every now and then, he wondered if he met the mark. How was Joe able to get to that point so quickly in our session? It was almost as though the thought had been resting on the edge of his heart and he just needed a place safe enough to expose his broken and vulnerable side.

If men were to be honest, they would *all* say that at some level they, too, have questioned whether they were man enough. Not necessarily to perform a particular task, but rather to experience the essence of what manhood really is. Joe was not only in crisis, but he was also acknowledging that manhood itself was in crisis. For Joe to survive, then manhood would have to survive with him.

The relationship Joe had with manhood was a serious and inseparable one. They had to win together. He could not live without manhood and manhood could not live without him. When God made him a man, He married Joe to the task of manliness and the seriousness of it as an integral part of his moral character. More than his marriage, more than his job, more than his kids, Joe wanted to know that he was "man enough." And when he could answer "yes" to that question, he would be more effective in his marriage, at his job and with his children. Joe needed to know what no one had ever taught him before: that he *was* "man enough."

Introduction: The Manhood Crisis

THE CRISIS OVERVIEW

The sad truth is that the vast majority of men are not manning up to their responsibilities today. As a result, not only have young men become a throw-away commodity, but great women, desperate for stable husbands, are at risk of never enjoying the one thing I believe everyone deserves an opportunity to experience: a solid family life.

The manhood crisis has reached a state of utter emergency. The causes of this crisis are too many and too rooted in centuries of sociological and cultural changes to delve into here. I have chosen rather to focus on where things stand today and identify the influences and pressures that modern society brings to bear on men and boys and what we can do about that. The decline of masculinity began a long time ago, but seems to be accelerating at an alarming rate in this first generation to come of age in the new millennium.

You may think that the word "crisis" is an exaggeration and that to say that manhood is in crisis is extreme. You may be of the opinion that there are men in crisis, but not manhood itself. And, yes, that's what I used to think as well. I thought that it was only certain men who could be identified as being in crisis. I thought that it was just the ones I saw abandoning their families and failing their children, their wives and their parents.

Then I looked more closely. I realized that my numbers had gone from the 30 or so men I observed personally, to 300, then to 3,000, to 30,000 and so on. I began to also notice how society views men and how the media uses what they know about men for mass marketing that speaks more to the degrading of manhood than it does to the products they are promoting. I wondered, "What do they really think about us?" "What do women really think about us?" "What do children think about us?" and, more importantly, "What does God think about our condition?"

I came to the conclusion that this is not just my problem; this is an American problem—no, a *world* problem. Manhood is in crisis! Men need to figure out how to bring it back from the brink and the women who love them need to figure out how to help their men do that.

THE RESEARCH

Incarceration Rates: "Young men who grow up in homes without fathers are twice as likely to end up in jail as those who come from traditional two-parent families...those boys whose fathers were absent from the household had double the odds of being incarcerated—even when other factors such as race, income, parent education and urban residence were held constant." (Cynthia Harper of the University of Pennsylvania and Sara S. McLanahan of Princeton University cited in "Father Absence and Youth Incarceration." *Journal of Research on Adolescence* 14 (September 2004): 369-397.)

Suicide: 63% of youth suicides are from fatherless homes. (U.S. D.H.H.S., Bureau of the Census. *See also* What Can the Federal Government Do to Decrease Crime and Revitalize Communities?, pg 11)[2]

Behavioral Disorders: 85% of all children who exhibit behavioral disorders come from fatherless homes. (*Id.*)

---

[2] "What Can the Federal Government Do To Decrease Crime and Revitalize Communities?" January 5-7, 1998 Panel Papers; a joint publication of National Institute of Justice and the Office for Weed and Seed; Oct. 1998, NCJ 172210, page 11.

Introduction: The Manhood Crisis

High School Dropouts: 71% of all high school dropouts come from fatherless homes. (National Principals Association Report on the State of High Schools.)[3]

Educational Attainment: Kids living in single-parent homes or in stepfamilies report lower educational expectations on the part of their parents, less parental monitoring of schoolwork, and less overall social supervision than children from intact families. (N. M. Astore and S. McLanahan, *American Sociological Review*, No. 56. (1991))

Juvenile Detention Rates: 70% of juveniles in state-operated institutions come from fatherless homes (U.S. Dept. of Justice, Special Report, Sept. 1988. *See also* footnote 3 below.)

Confused Identities: Boys who grow up in father-absent homes are more likely than those in father-present homes to have trouble establishing appropriate sex roles and gender identity. (P. L. Adams, J. R. Milner and N. A. Schrepf, *Fatherless Children*, New York, Wiley Press, 1984).

Aggression: In a longitudinal study of 1,197 fourth-grade students, researchers observed "greater levels of aggression in boys from mother-only households than from boys in mother-father households" (N. Vaden-Kierman, N. Ialongo, J. Pearson, and S. Kellam, "Household Family Structure and Children's Aggressive Behavior: A Longitudinal Study of Urban Elementary School Children," *Journal of Abnormal Child Psychology* 23, no. 5 (1995).

Achievement: Children from low-income, two-parent families outperform students from high-income, single-parent homes. Almost twice as many high achievers come from two-parent

---

[3] http://www.fathersrightsdallas.com/tag/national-principals-association-report-on-the-state-of-high-schools/#sthash.mtjinj0E.dpuf

homes as one-parent homes. (*One-Parent Families and Their Children*, Charles F. Kettering Foundation, 1990).

Delinquency: Only 13% of juvenile delinquents come from families in which the biological mother and father are married to each other. By contrast, 33% have parents who are either divorced or separated and 44% have parents who were never married. (Wisconsin Dept. of Health and Social Services, April 1994).

Criminal Activity: The likelihood that a young male will engage in criminal activity doubles if he is raised without a father and triples if he lives in a neighborhood with a high concentration of single-parent families. (A. Anne Hill, June O'Neill, *Underclass Behaviors in the United States*, CUNY, Baruch College. 1993).

THE CRISIS DEFINED

In every crisis there are four basic components: Conflict, Confusion, Opportunity for Change and Decision. These components interact with each other to create the dynamic of a crisis. In the case of the manhood crisis, I present the following.

1. Conflict

A conflict arises from two opposing factors. There may be several other elements contributing to the conflict, but ultimately there are two major forces at work. The major issue for conflict in the manhood crisis has been the shift in traditional male/female roles with the rise of feminism. A few generations ago, men were more responsible than they are now. They knew their place in society and willingly undertook the responsibilities that went with it. They also believed that

Introduction: The Manhood Crisis

women existed to give them moral and emotional support, to keep the home and raise the children, not to stand on their own as independent individuals.

Whether their motive was to fill the gap left by men who have escaped responsibility of the "manly stuff" or to answer the call of their own destiny, women have proven successful in filling traditionally male shoes. So what used to be a fight between a man and his world has now become a fight with his woman, because he feels the need to reclaim his role as head of the household, leader in the business world and major breadwinner from the one he thinks (rightly or wrongly) should never have had to take it over in the first place. I'm not insinuating that women must all return to being "barefoot and pregnant" as their only role in life; far from it. However, I don't necessarily see it as a disgrace to a woman if she has a man to take care of her and his family and she *chooses* in return to raise babies and keep a home. Women don't need Gucci shoes, business attire and a BMW to be seen as successful and accomplished. As a matter of fact, many of my female clients who have found success as professionals say they lack one thing that they want more than anything else: a good man!

So while it might appear that the two opposing factors are men and women, that would be an erroneous interpretation of the conflict. What is actually going on is that both men and women are struggling mightily to come to terms with the contradictions of old paradigms once imposed by society (and a grave misunderstanding of the tenets of the Bible) and the new roles a radically changed society now asks of them.

2. Confusion

Confusion is the feeling of not understanding something or not knowing what to do. No one really knows what to do about this manhood crisis. Men got confused to a degree when women started claiming their rightful/equal place in society; they thought they were losing something instead of seeing that they were really gaining something. Consequently, they became frustrated and angry and took that out on themselves (guilt as they saw their "power" waning) and those around them (jealousy and fear). You see, as women have taken lead roles in so many of the things we once considered "man stuff"—and in many cases are doing a much better job at it—men are left with feeling like they no longer have a meaningful role in society.

The women who love men don't know how to help them. Generations of men, raised by women, are relentlessly looking for other women to validate them. Churches are packed with women while some men find it "weak" to ask God for help. No one knows how to turn the table back towards responsible manhood, as laid out in the Bible, and every day seems to bring some new opinion or study with more ideas about gender, sexuality and gender roles which only add to the confusion. This leaves a befuddled man twisting in the wind of popular opinion and, in his desperate search for validation of his manhood, turning his manly love towards anyone for whom he's willing to sell his soul.

But when a man loves God, his wife, his children and his community and, in loving them, he takes responsibility for caring for them and entrusting that his impact in their lives is reflective of what God ultimately desires for them, then the confusion vanishes and he can truly call himself a man.

3. Opportunity for Change

The third component of a legitimate crisis is the opportunity for change. Does life present the opportunity to redefine manhood, and restore men's rightful place in the family and in society? I believe it does. I believe that the research data presented earlier poses not only the opportunity for change, but also the necessity of change. If we can overturn the failures that fatherlessness is causing, we will be able to re-establish the integrity of manhood around the world. But this will take making hard choices that may offend some people. We've got to be able to stand tall for men as leaders, protectors and providers of their families and economy. We have to give women the opportunity to get to know men the way men know men and the chance, ultimately, to love the men in their lives the way those men truly desire to be loved.

Thanks to the media, the internet and other resources, we live in a time when the world is an open book. Everything is available to us but that doesn't mean we need to succumb to the temptation to be open to everything. Because they are searching for their rightful place in society, men are most vulnerable to being influenced. However, just because we live in a world where it seems like anything goes, it doesn't mean that all things are fair game or that all opinions and ideas are equally good, valid or worthwhile. Not *everything* goes! Men need to examine their beliefs—about themselves, the world they live in and their relationship to God.

Men are beginning to see the light and wanting to reclaim their own rightful place in society, instead of dragging everyone around them down with them in their fear. They see that being stand-up guys who love and care for the people around them makes them more manly, not less. They see that the empowerment of women can also contribute to their own empowerment. This is their opportunity for change.

4. Decision

What decisions are we willing to make to lift manhood out of this crisis? What hard choices are we willing to make? What bold statements are we willing to make? What truth and convictions are we willing to stand on?

Are you willing to decide? Are you willing to do some thorough self-examination and then confront some hard truths about life, love and manhood that you probably would have never bothered to take a look at otherwise? Are you willing to decide to change the crisis now?

Well, I am. I will use the Bible to re-set the original plan for manhood. I will also use my background in psychology to address real, practical truths about manhood and human development. In my more than 18 years of working with men, I have uncovered the deep pains of manhood. I have put together this book by sifting through all the information gathered during those years, so that you can learn and discover things about men that will help you help them to regain their rightful position in the world.

In the following chapters, we will delve into issues such as what it is that makes a man "manly;" how the current crisis affects those characteristics; and what we can we do about it or, more specifically, what *women* can do about it. By the end of this book, you will have a blueprint or plan of action for putting an end to the crisis of manhood.

EFFECTS OF THE CRISIS

The effects of the crisis have impacted the character of manhood. The characteristics that make a man "machismo" or manly are severely influenced in four major areas:

Assertiveness: An ability to freely express his feelings, thoughts, and desires; maintain comfortable and emotionally balanced relationships; control his anger; compromise with others.

Responsibility: An ability to have an honest, insightful and self-reflective answer for his condition; to take moral and mental accountability for his lot in life.

Selflessness: An ability to think beyond himself and act outside of himself (unselfishness).

Respect: An ability to give regard to his whole self, to think, talk and act positively.

For men, these components are critical. Men like to believe that they possess them and are offended when anyone suggests that they don't. But in reality they are undeveloped in most men. Some of these characteristics are harder to acquire than others, but all of them are important. For example, a man who doesn't take responsibility for himself will never take responsibility for you.

Edwin Cole mentioned in his book, *Strong Men Tough Times*,[4] that Americans have sunk to new lows of lying, cheating and stealing, especially among the young. That trend is an obvious component of the disintegration of manhood. For a long time

---

[4] Watercolor Books (1993) p. 11.

now, the significance of manhood has been evaporating like the dew on a bright sunny morning. It is literally disappearing before our eyes. I believe the world is no longer interested in the contributions of manhood. Yet the world is so desperately in need of the contributions men can make to society! Sometimes the things you think you can do without are the very things that are needed to help you get to where you know you should be. Besides such factors as economic recovery, better schools and better paying jobs, we need strong God-fearing men who have determined to live and die with integrity. Men who know what it means to be a man and who make a conscious decision to progress in life with vigor and strength. Men who understand the real reason for their existence.

To bring resolution to the crisis of manhood, we must change how we raise and nurture the next generation of boys and young men today. We must begin helping them to become men who will to be productive; who will lead with integrity, credibility and excellence. I think children need it, women want it, and men are getting ready to embrace it.

A MAN'S ULTIMATE LIFE QUESTION

Men have a lot of questions about life, many of which they often don't talk about or even ask themselves about. Men have always been taught that they are supposed to have all the answers, so when it's time to ask questions they keep silent. During the last 18-plus years of working with men in therapy I have learned that men do have questions and they have *good* questions. They have questions that make you think, make you wonder and many times make you cry. They have questions that are simple and obvious and they also have questions that are subtle, questions they themselves don't even know they are asking through the way they act. These are the questions I want to talk about.

The biggest question all men have is, "Am I man enough?" Even though most men won't admit it, they do wonder whether or not they are "the man." Then, instead of digging deeper inside to find the answer, they look outside for proof and validation through sports, work, ownership of the most coveted new "man toy"—but, especially, they look to women. They want the perfect, most beautiful woman to hang on their arm, to gratify their need for pleasure, to feed their ego. Above all, they want to hear a woman say, "Baby, no one makes me feel like you do! *You're the man*!"

A man spends his entire life trying to ensure that he is in fact "manly." He wants to make sure that he measures up. Men do whatever it takes to prove that they are men. Most of a young boy's adolescence is spent proving to himself and his peers that he is a man. He hears messages about manhood through the media, music, schools, churches—just about everywhere. But his primary coaching regarding manhood comes from the family. Regardless of how much authority other ecological systems hold over him, there is something particularly influential about a boy's own family.

Boys learn to be men from the men who gave them life. Unfortunately in many cases, the men they learn from—if they are even around—have incorrect information. Thus, a young man must spend much of his life trying to unlearn what he learned wrong, or seek on his own other sources of information.

I once appeared before a classroom of inner city boys to give a speech on academic success. I knew that nearly 90% of the boys in the class were fatherless. I remember the look in their eyes as they gazed up at me. Although they asked about how much money I made, where I lived and what kind of car I drove, they were most concerned about whether or not I cared about *them*. They were hungry for men to care for them, to believe in them, to affirm the fact that they, too, were manly. I noticed how vulnerable they were, how needy they were, how willing to give and do anything to be affirmed as men. Then I recognized that I was no different—here I was, an adult male, seeking to receive a stamp of approval for my manhood from a room full of adolescent boys! Not only were their lives in crisis, but the man they were listening to was in crisis as well!

Since then, as I have observed other men mentoring young boys, coaching youth athletic teams, teaching in classrooms, running organizations and leading churches, I could see that they were dying inside because none of them had ever really figured out what it means to be a man. (I discuss this concept in depth in Chapter 15.) Stumbling over the superficial fragments of success with a wife, car, home, kids and church, they found no deep self-satisfaction because what they had come to learn about God never translated into what they needed to know about manhood.

That's the issue of manhood in the Church. Yes, boys were taught, for instance, that they were not supposed be gay, but they were never really taught how to be Godly, heterosexual men. "Don't be gay" somehow superseded "Be a man." It was more important to know about what you were not supposed to be than it was to know what you should be. The spaces between decisions of sexual immorality and the interpretations of real life experiences were lost and the results have been devastating.

For men, the real crisis is not the crisis of America, but rather the crisis of the Church in translating a life in Christ to a deeper understanding of what it means to men. I feel the Church plays a major role in painting the canvas for what a Godly man should be, but they never told us what to become. The focus was always on the negative—always on what not to do. We learned what not to do or what not to be but never what to do or to be. So by default we did nothing.

When I walked for the second time into that same classroom of boys with the same desperation for a role model—their eyes shiny and full of excitement and wonder, their hearts waiting and beating to the rhythm of "give me insight"—I told myself that, today, I would point them not to myself or the things that I have, but rather to a truth about why God made them men.

On this day, I would not talk about my car, school, college, money or my job. I would not discuss drugs, sex, education or bullying. Today I would discuss manhood, son-ship[5] and their reality. As I began to talk, my mind could not help but wonder what they were thinking about me. I was getting ready to tell them how great it is to be a man, how wonderful it is to be a son and how much responsibility comes with both those roles. I opened by saying, "Greetings, guys" just to get their attention and it worked—they all began to laugh at me! Little did they know that I was purposefully baiting them, hooking them in. How vulnerable they were. Tough looking on the outside, but so predictable on the inside.

These youngsters needed to hear something that day that would wake them up. So I continued, "Sorry, I mean, 'Whazz*up*?'" There! Now we were off to a better start.

I began telling them about some of the most difficult times in my own life, because they like tough hard stories—they're boys. Then I said something that caused them all to put their heads down and turn away from me. You could almost feel their emotional energy back away from the room into the safer depths of their hearts. What I said was, "My dad was not there for me." I said, "I don't know how many of you have ever wished you and your dad could be close, but for me he seemed so far away." I added emphatically, "I'm going to *make* him be my dad whether he likes it or not, because I feel like I deserve it." They smirked, but you could tell that they thought that was a pretty big proclamation.

As I was leaving that classroom, one of the young men came up to me. "Mr. Scott, I know exactly what you mean!" he said. "My father is in prison and I have not seen him. He murdered my

---

[5] We will be discussing "son-ship," as well as mentoring, in detail in later chapters.

mother when I was a little boy, so I went to live with my grandmother." The youngster told me how much he wanted to see his dad, how often he visited his mother's grave and how confused he was from all of it. Obviously, his story was more traumatic than mine and my heart began to break for him. Teachers would later tell me that this child never talked to anyone about that part of his life. "Bright" is what they called him. They excused his poor academic performance by suggesting that he didn't really apply himself the way he should. He was always getting into trouble, fights and arguments with other kids.

As crazy as it may sound, no matter that the man was in jail, I really sensed that this young man needed his father. He *wanted* his father, yet—digging even deeper into his feelings—behind all of that was his longing for *son-ship:* he wanted to *be a son*. He was undoubtedly a boy and a bit of a tough one at that, but he was definitely missing the affirmation of son-ship—something only his father could restore to him. Every time he tested his social system; every time he misbehaved; every time he did something that was risky, dangerous, and unreasonable, he was asking the question, "Am I a man now?"

This is the question most men project onto the women who one-day fall in love with them. It is a question that leaves judgment about the quality of manhood in the hands of the beholder. My objective is to get it out of those hands and back into their fathers' hands, where it belongs. God put something in every father that every son needs; when that son gets it, he realizes for himself how much of a man he really is. Then he never has to go looking for confirmation from women or from society at large.

> ³⁰ I searched for a man among them who would build up the wall and stand in the gap before Me for the land, so that I would not destroy it; but I found no one.
> **(Ezekiel 22:30)**

2

HOW MEN AND WOMEN THINK

HOW MEN THINK

"Is what I'm doing going to make me manlier?"

"Is what I'm doing sending the message that I am a man?"

A man has to have a real tangible reason to do something or he won't do it. Women can do things on a feeling. Men have to have a reason. The reason has to add credibility to their identity or they won't do it. Responsibility has to be reasonable before a man can ever accept it.

That's why it's so hard for men to stretch themselves out at the altar and cry and pray all day. They may want to, but they are always challenged with the question of what is it going to mean and what will be the benefit? Even if it feels right, sounds right, a man will still ask himself about the purpose of it. How is doing that going to look and what does it say about his manhood?

Appearances are everything to a man. You've got to understand that the way God created men, even when they're weak and scared they are wired to *look* strong. And if their appearance doesn't convince you that they can handle the pressure, they will do something to prove themselves.

So when you ask a man to do something, you have to tie it to something else that is affected by his doing it. For example, telling him, "If you work these extra days, your daughter will have the new dress she wants" is much more likely to get the desired result than just demanding, "You need to work more."

Have you ever noticed how irritated your man becomes when you tell him what to do or you suggest that he doesn't know how to do something? That's because men don't like being told what to do. And they like to think they know everything there is to know about everything. Most of all, they like being asked. Not only do they like being asked, they make sure you know that *they* are the ones who did whatever it was you asked for. They like getting your attention and hearing you say, "Thank you, baby!" for doing this or doing that. They like to hear you mention what they've done to your friends because that means you noticed the work they did. And when you notice the work they did, that means you're paying attention to them. Remember, men are easily intimidated and they are so needy in the area of personal attention! They think that if you don't mention the things they accomplished, it means you don't love them. They feel you don't care. They feel like they don't matter to you. It's just the way their brains work. So acknowledge your son and your husband every chance you get.

Men love to finish sentences for other people, especially those they are close to. It's a natural form of symbiotic attachment. When they really care about someone, their brains often jump in before they need to. They will think for you and speak for you. So when he tries to finish your statements, explain to you what you're saying, tell you how you should feel, or even try to fix you when you're not broken, it's because men think with their brains, not their emotions.

That's why love is so difficult for men. Love is often understood and expressed as fluid emotion or passion charismatically expressed without limit. This is very tough for men because they are so logical and calculating. Give him a fact, and he's fine. But add one feeling to that fact, and it equals a problem that must be fixed, because men see everything emotional as something that's broken before they see it for what it really is.

HOW WOMEN THINK (ABOUT MEN)

Rather than writing about *what* women think about men, I have chosen to write about *how* women think about men. There is a distinct difference. I believe women were created to talk and think with their bodies (feelings) not with their brains (logic). Women don't see into men's hearts right away. Women see the color of a man's eyes, his smile, his lips and, most of all, his attitude. Only then do they begin to see his entire body. Women don't think about having sex with a man as quickly as men think about having sex with women. First a woman thinks about what it would be like to be close to a particular man; to hold him, to be held by him. What would her body feel like next to his? What would it be like to touch his head or his hair? To put her hands on his face. What would it be like to walk with him or glance over the sea into a future with him? It's all body stuff, before it comes to sex. It's all feeling stuff. For women, the brain is not even working, but the body is in high gear.

Women even use their bodies to talk to men, too—body language. You change your walk, the way you smile, how long you look at a man. Women think of their bodies as magnets; you know men want to look at your bodies and are drawn to you by your bodies, so you use your bodies to do exactly that. You are correct; men do want to see female bodies. But what drives you to use your bodies is how you think about men—you don't think about men with your brains; you think about men with your bodies.

By the time a woman starts thinking logically about a man, he is often gone never to return. In the forward to his book, *Act Like a Lady, Think Like a Man*, Steve Harvey writes, "I want every woman…to forget everything she's ever been taught about men." But I'm not sure that a woman who thinks like a man would ever be able to act like a woman. Because the way you think and what you think with make all the difference. It's not only about sex, which is how this issue has been marginalized. It's more about the process of moving towards intimacy and how men and women get there.

WHAT WOMEN WANT FROM MEN

Men are not really interested in how women think about them as much as they are concerned with what women want from them. Most men think that women want their money or want to control them, but this could not be further from the truth. Women are not as complicated as men perceive them to be. The one thing women want the most from guys is probably going to be quite shocking to most men, and probably to some women as well.

Yes, a woman wants a man's protection; she wants to know that he loves her, she wants a man to pay attention to her, provide for her and lead her and the family. But that's not all she wants! Most of these things she can do for herself and many women are actually doing just that.

What women want is to have sex with men! Not just any sex, but GREAT sex!

That's right, I said it.

2: How Men and Women Think

Men have always gotten a bad rap about sex. We've heard for too long that sex is what men desire most, but that women can have it or go without it—take it or leave it. But the truth is, you want the same thing that society has chastised men for wanting, and you want it to be great, too. As a matter of fact, if you have it and it's not great—you haven't really had it.

When men and women accept this truth, it is going to change the way they interact—how they communicate with and respect each other.

Now, before you get the wrong impression, just listen to me for a minute! I interviewed more than 100 Christian women across the country, plus I've asked the opinion of more than 100 additional women who were being coached or counseled by me and 80% of them said that they wanted to have sex with their man after dating for less than 30 days. Most of them mentioned that they had been taught that this desire was the exclusive territory of men—that all men want from them is to get them between the sheets. So these women felt if they openly expressed their own desire, they would be stigmatized by society, to say nothing of the church. As a consequence, they had never been able to engage in an honest conversation about how much they wanted to have sex as well. Several of these women told me they knew within 15 minutes of a conversation with a guy if they were going to have sex with him. Let me remind you that these honest women were confessing Christians.

We need to take some time in this book to straighten all this out. I'll say it again: You women want to have sex and you want to have great sex. Notice, I didn't just say sex but, rather, *great* sex. "Great" is the qualifier. If you have sex and it is not great, then in a your mind you never really had sex at all.

So to the men I say: if you want a great woman in your life, you'd better find out what she means by great sex—and it could be different for every woman in the world.

SEXUAL ROLES—TRUE OR FALSE?

There are three basic things to be learned from this: the need for honesty; the value of conversation; and what even greater pleasures await when you wait for sex.

1. Get honest:

Society has shaped not only the roles of men and women but, also, how they should think of one another. Traditionally, men were cast as the breadwinners, the one who brings home the bacon, the leader in thought and politics, and the defender of the family and community. Women ever since Eve have been the helpmate, the nurturer, the raiser of children, secretary, nurse, teacher, giver and caregiver. When social norms are broken, roles are no longer determined by gender and people get honest, things change and we are better able to connect with each other.

Honest communication is the backbone of any good relationship.

One of the biggest challenges in marriages is sex. Couples just seem to lose their way after a while. More likely than not, this is because they have been living according to traditional social norms or outmoded societal expectations rather than being honest with each other. How often have you heard these lies repeated as if they were the truth:

"All men want to do is have sex."

"Women can take it or leave it."

2: How Men and Women Think

"The man should be the initiator and the aggressor."

"Women have sex for men and not for themselves."

And on and on—I'm sure you can add more.

I mentioned that women think of men with their bodies and men think of women with their brains. So it makes perfect sense that women want to have sex. Some women will read this and think, "Well, I want more than sex; I want connection and intimacy." And you probably do, but what you are referring to is the residual stuff that comes after great sex.

I guess a better way of saying it is that you want a man to stick around after having sex with you. So you fall for the old wives' tale that a "good" woman shouldn't want sex for sex's sake, but it's o.k. to use it as a hook. It's a way to catch a man. Society has convinced many of you that having sex just for your own pleasure means you must be loose or cheap, but that it's o.k. to have sex to please a man. So you hide your real feelings behind the mask of pleasing your man—pleasing him enough that, ultimately, he'll make a commitment. If he doesn't, then you regret that you gave your body to him. Society loads you down with guilt and you turn around and blame it on the guy. But who seduced who?

The truth is, women don't have sex with men *for* men. You honestly want to have sex for *yourself*, but if you fail to take responsibility for your own needs and the decision to have sex, you build a very shaky foundation for a relationship. Women need to be more honest and stop making men culpable for something that's not their fault. Guys, she did it because she wanted to. It wasn't to keep you. It was because she was just as sexually attracted to you with her body as you were to her in your brain.

2. Stop and talk about it:

When men realize that women are on the prowl for sex just like they are, they will have greater opportunities to observe for themselves that sleeping with a woman prior to committing to a long-term relationship has a dangerously powerful ability to draw both of them into emotional, psychological and spiritual connections that are way ahead of where they actually are in their relationship. One of the best conversations men can have with women is about sex, *especially when they are not having sex*. Because when a man and woman talk about these desires without satisfying them, they both gain a better understanding of how temptation works and get a hint of how wonderful sex could be. Great sex is one of the most beautiful things that can happen in a covenant relationship. Women want it from men and men want it from women.

3. Step beyond sex:

Once sexual desire of both parties has been "normalized," a man can start paying attention to the other needs of his woman because he no longer feels like he is the only one boiling with sexual passion. Unmarried couples can help each other remain celibate because they understand how much they *both* want to have sex. I once worked with a young lady who blamed her boyfriend for getting her pregnant and then leaving her, as though he did that by himself. She later began to take responsibility for her own sexual desires and sexual decisions; she then chose to be celibate until she married later on. When as a woman you take responsibility for the feelings society has taught that you should not want, you begin to free yourself to really live for God. You no longer have to pretend you don't want sex. That kind of game playing only sets you up to sleep with the next guy who fills your mind with dreams that turn false and promises made to be broken. Once a couple is married, a wife is free to express herself sexually and initiate sex as often as she wishes, without feeling guilty or slutty. Then, fulfilling your desires is one of the best gifts your husband can offer you, his wife.

Before you go off running and shouting through the house because you love that your healthy sexuality is finally being validated, let me pull you back just for a minute. Stop and think about it. Even though women want to have sex with men, there's also something they want to happen after sex. Women want and expect it and this is the thing that men don't understand. Men sell themselves short in their sex life because they don't engage in the gifts that come after great sex. They assume that the sex was it and they just start thinking of the next time. But women know that the greatest stuff comes after sex. They know that's the time when the brain opens to the heart— to dreaming, connection and exploring great possibilities together. That's why women want to cuddle and talk after sex— even though guys usually just want to roll over and go to sleep!

Men have four shortcomings that relate to relationships and get in the way of getting the blessings that follow great marital sex. They are: isolation, lack of trust, a heightened sense of sexual conquest and a lack of consistency. Men with heightened sense of sexual conquest don't give themselves a chance to reach a deep level of intimacy or ever experience real love, for that matter. When they are isolated and lack trust, they don't feel like someone could simply just love them. They project their own actions onto their partner and blame their partner for things they themselves are doing. When men lack consistency, they rob themselves of the power of rituals (doing the same thing the same way over and over again). They don't form the consistent habits that would allow them an opportunity to slow down and focus on the possibility of creating a lasting, fulfilling relationship with only one woman.

YOU DIDN'T MEAN TO TURN HIM ON

There is some level of narcissism in every man. As a matter of fact, a healthy dose of believing that you are "the man" can come in handy every now and then. But men need to be careful to control their ego because it can get them into trouble. For example, just because a girl looks at a guy doesn't mean she wants him. Just because she came into his office twice in one day, doesn't mean she wants to go to bed with him. Just because she went to lunch with him, doesn't mean she wants to spend the rest of her life with him. Men are always assessing whether a woman wants them are not. They gage most of their relationships with women that way—always thinking and always evaluating what a certain move by a woman means. Men are always looking for signs that seem to be pointing towards them.

You see, even though society has dictated that women shouldn't have carnal desires, every man wants to believe he is so irresistible that women just can't keep from being turned on by him. That's because most men are conceited and believe the world for some weird reason revolves around them. It's almost like she wouldn't be doing these things if he weren't there. Actually, that's how timid adolescent boys act—looking for the pleasure of sex without the commitment and the man stuff. These men may inhabit grown-up bodies, but they are really boys on the inside. They can't have fun without thinking that everything points to a woman being interested in them. To those men I say, "Grow up! She didn't mean to turn you on. Learn how to live your life connecting at another level and move away from the adolescent escapades that prevent women from viewing you and respecting you as a real man."

2: How Men and Women Think

> [23] The man said,
> "This is now bone of my bones,
> And flesh of my flesh;
> She shall be called Woman,
> Because she was taken out of Man."
> **(Genesis 2:23)**

3

HOW MEN MEASURE MANHOOD

- What is masculinity?
- How is it defined?
- What is the presiding paradigm of masculinity?
- How do we really know what manhood is?
- Who defines it and how is it measured?

These questions are important because the core issue of manhood depends on who has the right or who lives at a certain level (i.e., has the education, experience and or skill) to qualify him or her to define manhood or, better yet, to measure what manhood is.

The obvious answer to the last question is that God defines manhood. The Bible tells us:

> [1] How blessed is the man who does not walk in the counsel of the wicked,
> Nor stand in the path of sinners,
> Nor sit in the seat of scoffers!
> [2] But his delight is in the law of the LORD,
> And in his law he meditates day and night.
> [3] He will be like a tree *firmly* planted by streams of water,

> Which yields its fruit in its season
> And its leaf does not wither;
> And in whatever he does, he prospers.
>
> ⁴The wicked are not so,
> But they are like chaff which the wind drives away.
> ⁵Therefore the wicked will not stand in the judgment,
> Nor sinners in the assembly of the righteous,
> ⁶For the Lord knows the way of the righteous,
> But the way of the wicked will perish.
> **(Psalm 1:1-6)**

God is the only one who can truly set the parameters for measuring manhood. But the fact of the matter is that, while men may agree with this truth on the surface and usually "confess" it in public, in their minds they build their own personal definitions of manhood. And in defining it their own way, they also create their own rules for how it's measured—money, "toys," athletic skill, influence, power and control are the yardsticks they use. So instead of God being seen as the source and life of manhood, He is usually relegated to being just a guide for life in general.

So how does an ordinary, average guy measure manhood? What are some of the things that make him feel he is "man enough?"

- Strength, especially physical strength—does he have a muscular body? Is he a good athlete?
- Position and power—do people look up to him; are they afraid of him? Does he always have a pocket full of cash?

- Virility—can he satisfy a woman? Is he "the best thing that ever happened to her?" Can he demonstrate his virility by fathering a bunch of kids (even if he can't afford to support them)? Also, he can hold his liquor—even handle drugs with "no problem"— he thinks!
- Knowledge and skills—does he always put on a front of being right or knowing everything, even when he realizes inside it isn't true?

And then, what does a mature, Godly man think is "manly?" Does he ask himself if he's "man enough" to:

- Respect myself and keep on the strong and narrow path of a righteous life; take care of myself physically with exercise and healthy food; take care of myself spiritually with habitual spiritual practices?
- Love a woman for who she is and not what she can do for me?
- Show that love by respecting her, nurturing her ambitions, supporting her decisions and giving her physical pleasure?
- Love and respect my children enough to support them financially and emotionally; disciplining them with love and not just physical punishment (and *never* verbal or physical abuse); guiding them to build an intimate and strong relationship with God.
- Always approach life with courage, compassion and especially a sense of humor to carry me through the rough places?

The man that submits his will to God and sets his heart on the things God is pleased with is indeed a real man. Part of the challenge is that most men only have an intellectual concept of God with no real internal transformation of the heart. So men have to make the leap from their head to their heart.

When a man enters into a personal relationship with God through Jesus Christ, then God becomes first. Life becomes more introspective and his understanding is enlightened through how he fits into God's plan, rather than how God fits into his. Then God is not just an idea, but He is real and His realness is fully expressed through Jesus Christ.

Masculinity is twofold. It first has to do with what happens on the inside of the man. And secondly, it has to do with how what has happened on the inside affects him outside—how he presents himself to the world. Literally what he feels like and what he looks like or acts like.

What do we mean by what happens on the inside and outside?

"Are you a man or a mouse?" This is a challenge often thrown at a man whose physical or moral strength is being tested. Men are always passing judgment on other men: You're a mouse if you're scared and weak, a man if you're not. Then when he becomes a father, a man feels the essential thing to teach his sons is to never show weakness, even if they feel it deeply. Because that's what *he* was taught in the past. Maybe it was acceptable to show weakness to his momma, but definitely not to other boys or men.

So, most boys and men are conditioned to measure masculinity by how it appears on the outside when, in fact, it begins on the inside. Consequently, while the boy develops on the outside, inside he is screaming for answers to questions he refuses to ask out loud.

"Where am I?"

"Why am I here?"
"How do I become important?"
"What is my purpose?"

This internal drive coupled with confusion and internal confession motivates the man's actions. When a man confesses to himself that he doesn't know where he fits in or where he belongs, that he doesn't have all the answers to these demanding questions, it confuses him. He may present a strong face to the world, while inside he is screaming and no one hears.

The questions about the meaning of life must be answered. "I am material therefore I should seek material," they think; or maybe, "I am spiritual and should therefore seek spiritual" or even "I am both and must prioritize my existence." He must go inside to examine how he *feels* about that and then take *responsibility* for it. If he doesn't resolve these challenging questions for himself, he will forever seek to hide from his interior voices by turning to the women around him for answers.

The world's economic climate and dominant economic theories impact a man's thinking; he imagines that material gain and influence are more important than spiritual or moral gain. So most men would really rather be rich than be saved, or at least be rich when they are saved. That's because the philosophical influences, psychologically distorted images and references to manhood cause a man to struggle with status and success instead of dealing with issues deep in his own heart—issues that affect his thinking and his perception of who he is.

A man is an incomplete person until he becomes a fully-actualized, *Godly* man. What I mean by fully actualized is that he must develop a personal relationship with God that actually gives him insight and purpose for his existence. I mentioned earlier that this realization is two-fold. The first is spiritual and the second is psychological. A personal relationship with God that does not overcome the psychological distortions of a man's mentality secures his eternal life, but does nothing to change his personal life. So, salvation for the man is not enough. He must be a disciple. He must be taught, trained, loved and inspired in his natural life. I wish I could say that salvation alone automatically gives him that, but it doesn't; he actually has to work for that. Salvation is free, but discipleship will cost him everything. He will merely exist until he has discovered the purpose for his existence. Finding that purpose requires an accurate self- and sociological-measurement of himself. Where he comes from, where he is now and who or what is he being called to all become important questions that he must answer for himself. He must challenge the historical patterns of his family and create a new vision based upon the core principles of good moral standards in his own life. He must judge and re-evaluate the outcomes of his interactions and determine what he has done correctly and incorrectly. He must take responsibility for his own fears and his insecurities and face them with fearless faith. He must measure himself against himself, paying attention to his own ability and doing what it takes to enhance his own skills rather than comparing himself to other men. Again, it's all about making sure the measurements of his life are correct. Because when the measurements are incorrect, the pattern is wrong and the clothes—his "man suit"—just simply won't fit!

He must also prioritize his love life—loving God first, then himself and then others. The same type of progressive pattern is shown in his priorities and responsibilities (God's word, work and then a wife—in that order). A man's love for himself has to be balanced and put into the proper perspective. If he loves himself too much he will suffer from narcissism; if he doesn't love himself enough he will suffer from depression. He must love himself from the middle, between both extremes so that the rest of his love relationships are well balanced and he is able to discern what he needs to do in each system in which he is involved. That love must also progressively impact his world. It must spread beyond the confines of his own heart and head and be poured onto others. In other words he must find purpose in his life and pour himself out to that purpose until he is *empty*. In doing so he will experience great gain in both his life and the lives of others.

Although most men struggle with the "love" thing, it is imperative that they eventually "get it," because the essence of manhood is rooted in love and a man who can't love, can't really live.

Now, I know most men gauge manhood by other things than love and I want to take a look at the criteria they use.

Most men measure their manhood at three different levels: Status, Achievement, and Physical Risk. Let's review these levels and discuss the psychological impact this approach to self-evaluation can have on a man.

Status (how popular they are): Popularity is power. Men know that the more status you have the more power and influence you have and they are willing to do almost anything to get it. Men are natural born leaders so they gravitate to power and influence. When they feel powerless in certain situations, they often take it out on the people they know they can control (often their wives, girlfriends, children and parents).

Achievement (how much they have): That's right—a man's measure of his value is based upon how much he has. For boys, it's how many girls they've conquered—the more the better. For men, it's how much money they have made, because men measure their self-worth by looking at their net worth. They want a lot and they want it fast. The more broken a man is inside, the more he will try to fill this void with things.

Physical Risk (how brave and how bad they are): Don't give boys cake pans and baby dolls. Give them trucks, toy guns, dirt and rocks to throw. Boys grow up with a natural inclination to physical risk. They are "dare devils," as my grandmother used to say. They are always into something; jumping off furniture, slamming into walls, running in the street and—one of the things I had to discuss with my son when he was young—jumping off the house. The more physical and aggressive they are, the more manly they feel. Boys carry their risk-taking behavior into adulthood and use it to stand up for themselves in business, to get jobs, to defend their families and reputation and to invest in financial opportunities.

As you can see, nearly all of these self-evaluation strategies focus primarily on the "outside man" and have very little to do with a man's insides. Things like character, self-image, self-awareness, stability and integrity are not even part of the equation.

But this level of self-examination is a long way from where Man started. Do you remember when God created Adam from the dust of the earth? Well, His next human creation did not come from the earth, but actually came from Adam himself. God created Eve from Adam's rib (literally, from *inside* Adam, the birthplace of all future humanity). (Genesis 2:21) So men must remember that the greatest things in life come from the inside of who they are and not from the outside. If a man wants to maximize his life, he must do it from the inside. He must heal his soul, strengthen his spirit and transform his mind. Great things come out of him when he has done this.

The example of Eve being taken from the inside of Adam reinforces the truth that the opportunity for greatness lies within a man and cannot be obtained from things outside of him. The Bible tells us "He who finds a wife finds a good thing and obtains favor from the Lord." (Proverbs 18:22) But before a man can find a wife, he must first find himself because it is out of him that she is made and through his own eyes that she is seen. If he can get himself together, then and only then can she be made from him and found by him.

Man's (Adam's) first responsibility was to take care of the Garden of Eden. Men today also have a powerful responsibility: to take the good stuff they have within themselves and use it to cultivate the soil and plant the seeds of a healthy mind and soul in their children. The problem with many men is that they don't have anything of value to deposit because they are so empty on the inside themselves. Not knowing any better, they focus on the outside stuff, because that's all they've ever learned to identify with.

MANHOOD AND MADISON AVENUE

This is why men are so susceptible to the subtle or not-so-subtle tactics of Madison Avenue and why men are such a big market for high-end products. Marketing companies understand this so that's what they market towards. They use women and other sex symbols to market to men because it works. They advertise to the unconscious—going after what men mean rather than what they say. When a man says "I want a new car," what he's really longing for is to feel young and virile, attractive and powerful—without even knowing that those thoughts are operating at his unconscious level. So when he sees an ad that combines a sexy young female and a sexy car, he's not thinking, "That vehicle gets great gas mileage, will probably last a long time and has plenty of room for the kids, the dogs and the woman." He's visualizing himself at the wheel, feeling like "Yeah! I still have it!"

It's true, of course, that there are also plenty of ads for family cars and green cars—but guess who they are aimed at? You! The one in the family who keeps the wolf from the door by being realistic and practical. Not that women don't fantasize about driving sexy cars—they do. *When it makes sense*, they even buy them and drive them!

Marketing companies have also capitalized on the ultimate unconscious thoughts women have about men, and that's that men are stupid and easily persuaded. So advertisements often depict men in this manner. It's a sad reality, but it's true. Certainly, not all men operate at a purely unconscious level, either. But we're generalizing here to make a point. Until he changes the principles by which he lives, the average man can be walking around in a pretty unconscious state, still using sex, power and *things* to measure his manhood. As soon as men become conscious, the world around them will change and men will gain the respect they were created to have.

> [13] *Be on the alert, stand firm in the faith, act like men, be strong.*
> **(1 Corinthians 16:13)**

4

INSIDE A MAN'S WORLD

CREATION AS A MANAGEMENT OPPORTUNITY

Even though Adam was God's penultimate creation, everything He brought forth before that was created just for Adam. God created the world as a management opportunity for man. The world, though created first, would have had no real significance if it were not created specifically for the man.

What is the purpose of water, sunlight, day and night, trees, animals and the like if there is no person to appreciate it all? When you get to the fifth day of creation, you must ask yourself, "O.k., why all this stuff? What was the reason God created all these things?" Then you read that God created man and gave man dominion over everything so, in essence, the world was created with Adam in mind. The first had become last and the last had become first. Preparation had been provided and Adam moved into the neighborhood that God provided for him. It was all for Adam. No Adam—no creation.

FROM WOMB TO WORLD

The objectives of a boy's life are (1) to meet God, (2) to find a girl he can spend the rest of his life with and (3) to attain his dreams and goals, which now include the impact they will have on that special girl's life and the life of the family they create together.

"Boy meets girl" is still God's will—that "boy" should usher "girl" into her childhood dreams and help her make them a reality.

But this is not his first encounter with the female of the species. A boy isn't introduced to life by meeting a girlfriend, but rather he is introduced[6] to life by that most significant female: his mother. God does not first take a boy to a female, but rather brings a boy to his world through a female. That's right; it's through his mother's womb that he encounters the world. So, before he can know what woman to go to, he must first resolve issues related to the woman he came through.

Now let me pull him back a moment so that I can bring him forward. Let's talk about Momma.

A child begins to experience the plan God has set for his life as a man while he is being nurtured in the womb for nine months, totally cared for by his mother. As long as he is in the womb, a baby is dependent on the relationship his mother brings. His first field goal happens under her tutelage, his first three-pointer happens in her womb, his first punch, jump smile and flip all happen first in her womb. (My apologies for the rather heavy-handed sports analogy, ladies! I know your body is not a football field, but I'm talking about boys here and maybe some of you remember how hard those boys kicked!) Under her close watch, she feels his every move and she is attentive to all his activities until he is delivered from the womb to meet the world.

As warm and comfortable as it may be in the womb, God did not design children to stay there. The baby has to come out. If he didn't, both mother and child would die. God wants him

---

[6] Introduction (n.) late 14c., "act of bringing into existence," from Old French *introduccion*. *Online Entomology Dictionary* (Nov. 6y, 2013) www.etymonline.com.

there for a little while, but ultimately pushes him out into the world. The baby boy has to meet the world—it's the womb that enfolds him, but it's the world that wants him. And when the time comes, as safe as it may be in the womb, he *must* emerge—kicking and screaming—he must leave the womb to meet the world.

Again, the womb's purpose is to nurture the boy so that he may one day meet his world. In turn, this encounter with the world and his environment sets the stage for his curiosity about his Creator. The more conducive that environment is to helping him realize the need to know his Creator, the more accepting he will be of his need for a savior. It's the Creator question that stirs the salvation question. It's the need to understand the world that we live in that prompts the desire to be rescued from that same world. So, yes, Momma had to bear the initial nine months of her baby boy's existence within herself and by herself, but it was all because God wanted him in the world. Even if she wished she could nurture him that way forever, the relationship Momma has with her child is designed to shift. And this shifting will involve her pushing him away from her—which is a dynamic I will talk more about.

Now, leaving the womb does not come easy. Whether it's natural childbirth or Caesarean, it's a traumatic journey. And it doesn't stop with being taken from the womb—the baby actually has to be cut away from Momma. His first encounter with independent life is the moment he takes that first breath. The intake of oxygen and the release of carbon dioxide. An exchange between him and the plants of the Earth. But just as he has to breathe on his own, he also needs to be nourished through his mouth instead of the umbilicus. Imagine that, he's breathing independently but still feeding on his momma until that cord is cut. Their relationship is iconic and spiritually extraordinarily amazing!

So, he goes from the complete dependence in his mother's womb to interdependence with the world. He takes something (oxygen) and returns something back (carbon dioxide). A child's first worldly experience is anchored in *sowing and reaping*—a principle of management that is necessary for the rest of his survival. Real men live under this principal of sowing and reaping because their entire life is based upon it. Real men know that if they don't deposit anything there won't be anything available for withdrawal. They don't expect to get back what they have not put in. They also recognize that they should be careful about where they put things because the result of putting things in the wrong place could be no harvest at all (i.e., no reaping) and that might even cost them their life.

As I will discuss in Chapter 5 on sexuality and sexual struggles, since a boy comes from the womb, he will always want to return to the womb. He will always be looking for that place of safety; that place that gave him opportunities to be vulnerable, free and taken care of. Once he transitions from the womb to the world, he is vulnerable to the pressures of the world, which may send him running back. And the harder life becomes, the greater that urge becomes.

Even though the doctor has cut the umbilical cord, a man who is reluctant to be out in the world may still keep the cord tied tight to his heart. Such a man has probably not been sufficiently pushed and called[7] so he continues to be dragged around through life by his mother. She is in his business, his relationships and his money. He can't seem to grow up because she can't seem to let him go. Often a man like that will enter into relationships with women who feel sorry for him. He will use guilt to get what he wants and pity to keep it.

---

[7] See Chapter 7—The Importance of Being a Son for discussion of "pushing and calling."

FROM WORLD TO GIRL

A man who has not successfully mastered his world will have major problems mastering his relationship and the way he engages in that relationship. When life is out of perspective then love is out of perspective. He has to resolve his "worldly" encounters to figure out how to engage in "girly" encounters. If he doesn't, he will drag his girl through a world of heartbreak, problems and pain. His insecurities, lack of focus, greed and fantasy will drive her from being his woman to trying to be his mother (if she sticks around). She will have to parent him on the one hand and have sex with him on the other. In the process, she will get confused, depressed and discouraged; losing her identity, herself and the man she loves.

Life should happen in an order that leads to God's ultimate objective. A man should develop and progress in three distinct phases: Worship, Work and Wife, in that order. In essence, the world he discovers should move him to *worship* God and to manage the world by his *work* for God. Once he has done this, he is ready to find his *wife*. A man who is stuck in immaturity tries to jump over the worship stage and sometimes even work, to look for a wife. And when he has done this, consciously or unconsciously, he assigns his woman the task of healing and restructuring his whole perspective. He will be hard to get to, difficult to understand, complicated and most often emotionally detached. Here is why:

We often think of men as lacking in responsibility, but in reality what they do and what they want are two different things. There is this gap between their wants and their actions. Your objective is to help men get what they want. As you think of the man or men in your life, think about them in this way and decide how you can be most effective in helping them get there—which, in some cases, means leaving them to themselves until they figure it out! The responsibilities and demands of life scream at men like an abusive parent or slave master, insult them and blame them for not being men, as though they are what create the man. It's just plain hard!

In order for men to survive in this world they must find the place that offers them a few basic things. These things are to a man's soul like food and water are to the body.

1. Men need **belong** to something. Men want to feel they are part of something bigger than themselves. They want to be able to influence the movement or progression of something. They want to be needed and needed in a way that makes them accountable; a way that makes them feel like they have ownership.

2. Men need **respect**. Men must feel a sense of respect, because when a man feels respected, he feels safe. And when men feel safe, they function better. A man would rather you respect him and not love him than to love him and disrespect him. For men, the hallmark of love is respect. They don't understand love without respect. They place respect higher than love.

    Men are sensitive and deeply insecure because their calling by God is so high. There is no calling in scripture higher than loving your wife "as Christ loved the church." By nature men are placed in a position of intense and passionate accountability. So, in general, men are fearful. They fear that they are not cutting it in life. They have hard times with breakups and "moving-ons." As a matter of fact they treat a relationship with someone who decides to move on like a breakup. They treat a lost job like a break up. Their vulnerability leads them to misinterpret difficult challenges as attacks on their character and their person. That's why respect is so important. Respect reaches down into the depths of who they are and lets them know that you understand them. That you love them. And that you consider them as most important. Men need that.

3. Men need **affirmation**. Men need to know that they are o.k., literally. Affirmation is a fancy word for "I know and accept all of who I am and all I am ever to be." A sense of affirmation is one of the feelings a father gives to his son. Because boys struggle psychologically as they develop in their quest towards personal identity and worth, they need a man to affirm that all they are going through internally is normal and necessary. Otherwise they will feel like something is wrong with them. They will begin to reject the part of themselves that produces shame and guilt, like masturbation or wet dreams. As his body grows on the outside, the little boy on the inside has to grow with it.

Inside himself, a maturing boy knows he's being called to lead. But he's also had a dream that gave him a feeling of euphoria and he struggles to chase the "high" produced by that dream. He wants that feeling again at whatever cost.

Being affirmed calms down all of those feelings in boys. It sits the emotions down so they can be examined and helps the young man realize that the end of boyhood is not the end of the journey. Affirmation is a powerful tool that can be used to reach deep into the subconscious and call it to consciousness, waking the boy up and letting him know he is not alone. Unfortunately, many men have not been affirmed by other men. Therefore, a woman has to spend emotional energy trying to show him how she appreciates him because she can never give him the kind of affirmation he should have received from his father or other men. When you appreciate, encourage and support your man, it helps him to heal from the scars of not being affirmed as a boy.

4. Men need **projects**. (I'll bet this one comes as a surprise!) Ladies, don't let your man go without projects. As a matter of fact, don't even let your *sons* go without projects. Since men like projects, there always has to be a problem for them to fix. If there isn't one, they will create one. And sometimes that could be you! How often have you felt as if your man were treating you like an assignment or a task? Like he's trying to figure out how you're designed; trying to read your blueprint. So, if you don't want to be fixed or overhauled, make sure you have plenty of other projects for him.

Keep his "Honey Do" list full! Because, whether you realize it or not, completing projects for you is BIG for him. I remember cutting my mother's yard when I was about 10 years old. Every weekend my routine was to get up and cut the yard, wash the car and clean the driveway. I loved doing it. I got energy from working hard. I *thought* it was about work ethic. I *thought* it was about being a man. But now I realize it wasn't. My mother would come out and look at the yard or the other jobs and smile. She'd fix me an ice-cold coke and bring it to me as though I was a man. It wasn't the work I loved so much. It was the smile, the ice-cold coke and the idea that my mother needed me for something. For a man to know that you need him is a gift to him. To make him feel you don't is like a curse.

5. Men need to feel **loved** and **desired**. Notice that I said they need to "be loved" rather than they want to be "in love." Unlike women, men want to be the object of love rather than giving themselves to it. It's just the way they are wired. In fact, it is sometimes hard for a man to say he loves you, but he is always expecting you to tell him that! When a man feels like you don't desire him he will quickly shut down towards you and consider another woman. First, he will think that you are cheating; then he'll check out. Men love to feel desired. This is so underrated! Society usually attributes the need to feel desired to women, but men need it just as badly.

    Men need to see signals that indicate you want them. When a man looks at you in the mall, he gauges his interest in you not so much by what he sees as by whether or not you look back at him, and what he *thinks* your look implies. Men are so needy in the area of desirability that they often get the cues women give them confused and assume that the slightest bit of attention means you want them, or at least you want to have sex with them. That's because their antenna for attention and being desired is so high it misreads other signals. Sex for men is also predicated upon this principle. When a man has sex with you, he interprets that as "you want me." Not "you love me," but "you want me." A man rarely tells you how much he loves you when he's having sex with you, but he does want to hear how much *you* want *him*—even to the point of hearing you call out his name during sex. Men love themselves; their sex life and personality are ego driven. It's the way God created them. A confident woman who sends clear and appropriate signals can help a man become more vulnerable and increasingly selfless and giving.

*⁹ How can a young man keep his way pure?
By keeping it according to Your word.
¹⁰ With all my heart I have sought You;
Do not let me wander from Your commandments.
¹¹ Your word I have treasured in my heart,
That I may not sin against You.
¹² Blessed are You, O Lord;
Teach me Your statutes.
¹³ With my lips I have told of
All the ordinances of Your mouth.
¹⁴ I have rejoiced in the way of Your testimonies,
As much as in all riches.
¹⁵ I will meditate on Your precepts
And regard Your ways.
¹⁶ I shall delight in Your statutes;
I shall not forget Your word.*
(Psalm 119:9-16)

5

HIS SEXUALITY & SEXUAL STRUGGLES

Have you ever wondered why some guys you date seem to only want to have sex with you? Why every time you want to talk, they want to touch? Why when you want a relationship, they just want a romantic moment or two, or three or…?

Why did your mothers and grandmothers tell you that boys only want one thing? Well, I can say this: They were right. Boys are driven to want one thing and one thing only. They want sensation. Not necessarily sex, but they want a feeling, stimulation. Long before they reach adolescence, they have already learned to stimulate themselves through masturbation. They are males and males have the disquieting attribute of having their genitals exposed—bam! —right there in front of them. A phallus is a pretty amazing work of creation, because it gets large (fills with blood without clotting, which is a miracle!) and then goes back down—sometimes for no reason.

Boys don't have the privilege of having their genitals hidden like girls do. They don't have to figure out ways to stimulate themselves—the wind can blow and their "thing" goes acting up again. A look, a touch, a thought or any simple thing can send them rushing to compensate for what could be deemed very "inappropriate behavior"—even though it was beyond their control. Boys learn to live with the reality of spontaneous sexual stimulation as children and their bodies are their very first toys because they are so handy! Like it or not, there is power in the penis and a male spends his entire young life exploring what it can do and then later learning to contain and control that power.

Boys need to know that—in spite of the power their penis seems to hold over them—they are normal, that there is nothing wrong with them. They need to know that they are not sexual monsters or angry beasts just because the sensations and temptations that they experience are much different than that of girls. Boys need to know that the responsibility they have is to learn how to manage their sexual temptations is all part of becoming a man.

A BOY AND HIS MOTHER

It's really *easy* for a boy to love his mother. There is something innate in the relationship that just gives him permission to love mom. Boys just love their mothers. I mean, mom can make him angry, discipline him and tell him "no" for everything and he is still attached to her. As a mother, you can get away with things that fathers can never dream of getting away with. It is harder for a boy to express love to his father than it is to show love to his mother because, once a boy is no longer a baby, a son needs his father the most. But that transition to eventual manhood is tough, so the boy gravitates towards what is easier (mom) rather than the hard journey through son-ship with his father to guide him.

A mother has a special relationship with her son, a relationship that is sometimes so enmeshed the boy is never able to grow away from her womb. That's right, that's what I said. Boys can remain attached to the umbilical cord even after it's been cut. As adolescents, many boys go from girl to girl and later from woman to woman as men, all the time looking for the confirmation of the womb. As men struggle with very difficult

5: His Sexuality & Sexual Struggles

times in life, they often think of being held by their mother. The womb is the safest, most silent place a male has ever known, and his deep, subconscious thought is of actually returning to the peace and tranquility of the womb.

As a mother, your job is to push your son out your womb and away from you into life. So, yes, boys actually need to be called from their mother's womb at some point in their life, preferably when they start to develop testosterone and make physiological transitions into adulthood. Remember, it's all about making him a son; about allowing him to *be* a son, because there is no better bridge to manhood than son-ship.

There is a story in scripture that is easy to skim over without paying real attention to the insight to be gained from one of the richest and smartest men encountered by Jesus. The guy was a Pharisee, a well-respected leader and considered to be a great teacher. And great teachers normally ask great questions.

The man's name was Nicodemus and his story is related in the Gospel of John (John 1:3). One evening Nicodemus asked Jesus what he needed to do to inherit the Kingdom of Heaven. Jesus responded that no one can see the kingdom of God unless they are born again.

"How can someone be born when they are old?" Nicodemus asked. "Surely they cannot enter a second time into their mother's womb to be born!"

Nicodemus' response is startling because it hints at the possibility that a man might re-enter the womb. From a distance it seems a bit silly, but a closer look at his response gives us insight into the role of mothers and power of the womb. Nicodemus responded as though the only thing that can give birth is the womb—as though the womb must be the source of all life and hold the keys to Heaven. As though there is no way to be born—even born *again*—into anything unless the mother's womb brings it forth. To Nicodemus' way of thinking, in order to get to an eternal state of peace with God, you would have to re-enter the womb that had provided the most peaceful environment any man ever experiences.

Today, many men want to return to the womb because they basically still haven't grown up. They want the comfort of Momma's womb and that makes it difficult for them to really come to know God. Realizing that the only way to the womb is through a vagina, they seek woman after woman, sexual relationship after sexual relationship, trying to find comfort by filling the gap with sex. But sex doesn't save them and in this state of mind even the greatest sex leaves them unsatisfied and looking for the next best experience. This only leads to frustration, because they will never find it. They try to resolve their problems with each new sexual experience, not realizing or unable to accept the fact that their rebirth will never be in the womb, but rather in the Spirit.

Nicodemus asked the question and Jesus gave the answer: "Very truly I tell you, no one can enter the kingdom of God unless they are born of water and the Spirit. [6] Flesh gives birth to flesh, but the Spirit gives birth to spirit. [7] You should not be surprised at my saying, 'You must be born again.' [8] The wind blows wherever it pleases. You hear its sound, but you cannot tell where it comes from or where it is going. So it is with everyone born of the Spirit."

Yes, Nicodemus was thinking "fleshly," but he was also right in thinking that when a man doesn't come to know God through the Spirit, the only god he can know is his mother and the only Heaven he can imagine is Momma's womb to which he will never be able to return.

5: His Sexuality & Sexual Struggles

When a man realizes this, he stops having indiscriminate sex and begins to dedicate himself to God, using his body to glorify God in the Spirit. He discovers that worshipful experiences are even better than the safety and comfort of his mother's womb.

What also happens is that he begins to look for his father. A man making this transition realizes that the womb was only an incubator where the seed he came from rested. Thus, when men see beyond the womb, they truly find God and begin looking for their father to affirm them as a son.

As a mother, it's important that you understand that your son must make this transition for himself. Momma can do a lot, but she cannot do that. As a wife, if you see that your husband is only now realizing that he must make this transition, you can gently encourage him to change the nature of his attachment to his mother (or you, as his surrogate mother) and seek out a healthy relationship with his father.

Be forewarned, however, that you may encounter some choppy waters here. When a man recognizes that he has been tied too long to the apron strings, he may overreact and push too far, trying to control his woman because he doesn't want her to control him. This is why "liberated" women feel like such a threat to his manhood. The slightest inclination that a woman is attempting to run his life makes him nervous and he defends himself the only way he knows how. The old paradigm has affected him by making him scared, intimidated, insecure and fragile—all because he has never been pushed and called.

Just as men can use money or muscle to control their women, women—unfortunately—sometimes use the power of the vagina to control their men. This is because a man who is more inclined to the "easier, softer way" will seek the comfort of the womb (sex) rather than heeding the more challenging call to son-ship and manhood.

A grown man doesn't deserve to live this way and he's got to find a way out. Hopefully, he will discover that son-ship is the room where he needs to live for a while and God is the door through which he must pass to enter. He needs to find his father. Confront his father. Forgive his father. He needs to emotionally connect to his father because he is his father's seed. Being my father's son does not make me turn into my father. It only means I know where I came from and I accept what God has created through my dad.

You can best help your man by loving him "beyond the womb." Love him in a way that shows him there is more to you than sex. Help him understand that love can be found in the heart and safety can be held in the hand. Your sex life will become so much more meaningful when you understand how hard it is for a man to move beyond his mother. If you don't do this, you will always have to compete with other women, wonder about other women and even feel like you are raising a boy in man's body. You need to be a wife, not his mom. He needs your help to tell Momma bye-bye and say hello to a woman, a wife, and a friend—you!

5: His Sexuality & Sexual Struggles

> ² *What, O my son?*
> *And what, O son of my womb?*
> *And what, O son of my vows?*
> ³ *Do not give your strength to women,*
> *Or your ways to that which destroys kings.*
> ⁴ *It is not for kings, O Lemuel,*
> *It is not for kings to drink wine,*
> *Or for rulers to desire strong drink,*
> ⁵ *For they will drink and forget what is decreed,*
> *And pervert the rights of all the afflicted.*
> ⁶ *Give strong drink to him who is perishing,*
> *And wine to him whose life is bitter.*
> ⁷ *Let him drink and forget his poverty*
> *And remember his trouble no more.*
> ⁸ *Open your mouth for the mute,*
> *For the rights of all the unfortunate.*
> ⁹ *Open your mouth, judge righteously,*
> *And defend the rights of the afflicted and needy.*
> **(Proverbs 31:2-9)**

6

THE ROLE OF MOM AND DAD

I know there has been a lot of discussion around the importance of fathers in the lives of their children—especially when it comes to the lives of their sons—and in large part that is what this book is about. Research on the issue is fairly consistent and the experiences many boys have had because of an absent father are pretty similar. So who do they need most, Mom or Dad? And what do they get from each?

That's what I plan to address in this chapter. My ultimate purpose is not to use research to defend one side of the argument or the other, but to give you a very practical perspective to provoke you to begin thinking through this issue in a different way. The "absent father" issue seems to be what interests most people about *this* generation. I admit this surprises me because in past generations where fathers *were* present, their role seems to have been taken for granted and their importance rarely discussed.

Let's look at what we do know. We know that it takes a man and a woman to create a child. We know that it is God's intention that children be born as a result of the joining together of the egg of a woman and the sperm of a man. So the real issue is not about the parents' role in creation but, rather, in development. The big question is "Now what?" —which is the very question most people fail to answer. Like when you went down the aisle in church to get saved and then it was, "O.k., I'm saved. Now what?"

Once a child is born, what needs to happen between these two people to shape their child's personality into the most wholesome, healthy and productive person possible? What is the role discipline plays? Do abuse, arguing and abandonment have an impact? Does divorce have an impact? And is there a difference between what Mom and Dad each bring to the table?

I would like to propose a new paradigm. It is a working paradigm based on over 18 years of my private practice and extensive experience treating individuals and families. My view is also based on the personal consequences in my own life of divorced parents and an emotionally absent father, which I will reflect on in this chapter.

Most of what I say here is supported by the research. However, parenting is not a concrete science, although it lends itself to the science of psychology and is impacted by both genetics and the childhood environment. We will try to remain as logical and practical as possible, so that you will gain useful insights, rather than just the debatable theories of research.

Here we go!

Every boy needs the following things to support his healthy overall development:

- Love
- Affirmation
- A Sense of Belonging
- Support
- Appreciation

- Discipline
- Respect
- Safety

You can see that this list is very similar to our list in an earlier chapter of what *men* need. I will not focus on the basic necessities of life such as food and water, clothing and shelter, assuming that loving parents provide these to their children. The things in this list are more fluid and less tangible; they help to shape the personality and the self, rather than the physical body. They have influence on the psyche of the boy and eventually inspire or hinder him in defining for himself his purpose, passion, hope and the development of self-esteem, self-image and self-worth. You may be able to list other things, of course, but they will probably fit into one of these broader categories.

Since we are saying that all boys need the above, the question is which parent is best equipped to deliver each of these elements of well-being to their boy? A sample question to ask yourself might be: can Mom give love to her son? The next would be: *does* Mom give love to her son or should that be something Dad does, while Mom focuses on giving him other things on the list? I think the answer to that particular question is quite obvious. Mom can and should give love to her son. Well what about Dad? What does he need to do? Again, Dad can and should give love as well. So the issue is not whether we need to divide up these basic concepts of human development and give some to the mom and some to the dad. The real issue is not what each parent gives, but rather *how* they give it.

That's right. I am proposing that both parents can and should give love to their son. The big difference is in the way they do it.

Let's go back to God's original design, which we talked about in the beginning of this chapter. God gave your son a mother and a father. He comes from a man *and* a woman, and each of them can and should deliver the necessities for healthy development. The woman can deliver them, but not same way the man does; and the man can deliver, but not like the woman. When both parents are present in a boy's life, he receives love and discipline from each one in their own unique way. Children from single-parent homes don't lack the basic developmental necessities by having only one parent present, but they miss the other side of the instruction and that hinders them. If one parent (most commonly, the father) is missing, it isn't that the boy doesn't receive these necessities, but he will only be getting them from one side in spite of every effort on the part of the parent who *is* present to fill the gap.

We are not dealing with gender roles and parenting styles here, but addressing parenting's spiritual aspects of cutting through life with a *double-edged sword*. I would like to use this analogy to further develop my point. That double-edged sword is mentioned many times in the Bible; in Hebrews, for example:

> *[12] For the word of God is living and active and sharper than any two-edged sword, and piercing as far as the division of soul and spirit, of both joints and marrow, and able to judge the thoughts and intentions of the heart.*
> **(Hebrews 4:12)**[8]

---

[8] See also: Judges 3:16; Psalm 149:6; Proverbs 5:4; Revelation 1:16 and Revelation 2:12.

6: The Role of Mom and Dad

We are totally dependent upon God at the same time that we are interdependent on one another and the world at large. This concept of the double-edged sword for a child's development points us to the need to have two active parents, because each parent will render what is needed from a different point of view— a different side of the sword. The mother will cut one way and the father will cut another way. The intention is for them never to be the same; rather, it's the differences that the boy needs the most. Let's look at an example.

Corey's Story

Corey's mom and dad separated when he was 11 years old. Corey knew that his mother and his father both loved him very much. He knew that they would each do anything for him. So he enjoyed spending time with both of his parents. But after a while Corey sensed his dad changing towards him; his father thought Corey was beginning to side with his mother and was defending his relationship with his mother. As Corey grew older, this tension only grew worse between father and son. Not surprisingly, he grew much closer to his mother. The only time his mother ever discussed Corey living with his father was when he started getting into a little trouble during high school. Although she loved him very much, her love, as explained by Corey, was "soft."

"She fussed a lot and yelled at me. There were times she had gotten so upset with me that she pushed me and started crying. She made me feel like I was hurting her. She made me feel like I was breaking her heart and she wanted me to stop. I felt so guilty. I knew in my mind that I didn't want to hurt her. I knew that I loved her. I would think about all the things she had been through and sometimes that made me angry. Part of me wanted to stop her from crying; the other part was angry and wanted to leave. I always lived between the tension of loving her and leaving her. I felt I needed to take care of her. I felt emotionally responsible for her. I was her son, but something inside me felt like I was just as responsible to her as a husband should be."

Because his mother cared for him very much, Corey grew up with one of the greatest elements of development necessary to young boys: love. However, his mother's love was very emotional and sometimes overly entangling—as he said, "soft." The result was that Corey felt responsible for her.

Most mothers love that way. They love deeply; *emotionally* deeply. Their love is real, it's personal and it can make the loved one(s) feel responsible for the relationship. A father's love is quite different.

Remember, there are two sides to the sword: one side the mother's and the other the father's. Corey was missing the father's side of love, the side that would balance him and push him emotionally to the middle.

Fathers normally reflect on consequences in the outside world. They tend to focus on how behavior affects others and not themselves. Their love is usually less emotional and more logical than the mother's. Fathers attack the brain and use words—sometimes too many words—to express love. Fathers are more apt to become physical with their sons. They get angry sometimes because they love their sons. This can be scary for a mother. She doesn't love like that, so she doesn't understand it. But these two sides of love help the child stay balanced and become more capable of handling the outside world.

6: The Role of Mom and Dad

Here are a few other examples of how mothers and fathers express themselves in different but equally important ways to their children:

- Love
  - Mom: Affectionately looks at her son and smiles.
  - Dad: Sets overly restrictive curfew.

- Affirmation
  - Mom: As a female, interacts with him in ways that teach him he is a male.
  - Dad: Interacts with him physically, aggressively; but hangs back and lets things play out before rescuing him.

- Sense of Belonging
  - Mom: Shows affection.
  - Dad: Makes him responsible for upholding the family name.

- Support
  - Mom: Comforts and nurtures him when he is in trouble.
  - Dad: More focused on dealing with the threats than dealing directly with him.

- Appreciation
  - Mom: Hugs him and praises him when he does well.
  - Dad: Tells him what he could have done better or should do next time (if there *is* a next time!). Gives him approval to go on.

- Discipline
  - Mom: Sets boundaries, but bends the boundaries for convenience.
  - Dad: Overreaching in boundary setting.

- Respect
  - Mom: Wants him to respect himself.
  - Dad: Wants him to respect others.

- Safety
  - Mom: Ensures that he knows her presence makes him safe.
  - Dad: Focuses more on the environment and making sure the environment is safe even when he (Dad) is not there.

In working with couples, I always help them understand that their differences are necessary in the effective parenting of their children. I remind them that the better they are at trusting they both have the child's best interests at heart, the better the child is going to be. Just because mothers and fathers are different and each apply a different side of the sword in child rearing doesn't give either of them an excuse *not* to do some basic things very necessary for helping sons build strong self-esteem and self-image. Here is a list of things parents should say to their sons *regardless* of whether they are the mother or the father. Boys need to hear these phrases over and over growing up and, if they do, they eventually begin to believe them:

- "I believe in you."
- "I am proud of you."
- "I love you."
- "You matter to me."

These are the words I call "man words." I know they are important for daughters, too, but *God* do they do something to the inside of a boy!

6: The Role of Mom and Dad

PUSHING AND CALLING

Now that we've gotten that under our belts, let's talk about (1) the one thing that women *cannot* do for sons—that only a father can do, and (2) the only thing a mother *can* do that a father cannot do. It's what I call "pushing and calling." I briefly touched on this previously in the chapter on sexuality and I will discuss it in more detail in Chapter 7—The Importance of Being a Son. The idea is that a mother's ultimate objective for her son is to be able to push him towards his father at the same time the father calls his son to himself. As the father calls him and the mother pushes him, the boy is forced from the womb of his mother to the bosom of his father. He is pushed from the comfort of emotional support and nurturing and pulled to the challenge of the playing fields of life.

> [6] *Train up a child in the way he should go,*
> *Even when he is old he will not depart from it.*
> **(Proverbs 22:6)**

THE IMPORTANCE OF BEING A SON

"Be a man!" "Be a man!" "Be a man!"

That's all I heard growing up. And I *got it*. I figured out that I needed to be a man, whatever that was. I knew that there was a transition from the boy I was to the man I would become. What I didn't know was that there was something between the two and nobody was telling me to be what was in the middle.

As I tried to break through the eggshell of my mother's love and become a man, I often felt like falling back into the egg because my legs were weak, my mind was unprepared, my heart was broken and the examples I saw around me of supposed manhood terrified me. I knew that something was wrong. I observed that men were inconsistent, saying one thing and doing something else. They were gossipers, always finding a tree to get under to talk about nothing. As a boy I knew something was wrong when I would see a living room set under a tree (the couch, the chairs and, oh, all those empty bottles!). These men were cowards—afraid of commitment and deep relationships. They would rather fist fight than fight for years to grow a strong business. They were delusional—believing they were what they were not and had what they did not have. They were liars—they lied to everybody about everything. They were religiously destructive—going to church for all the wrong reasons. But now, as an adult myself, I realize that they were men just trying to figure out how to *be* men. And that's all they knew to say: "Be a man!"

So as I grew up, I dressed like a man; looked like a man; talked like a man. But deep inside, I was empty. Because I had been a boy and I had become an adult, but I had never ever been a *son*. I had never experienced that period of son-ship that should have taught me what being a man was truly all about.

The phrase "I am my father's son" seems to have gotten lost in the wave of fatherlessness and the lack of honor fatherhood has held lately. There are more young men proud to be their momma's boy than their father's son and rightfully so. So many mothers have had to raise children alone because of the increase in out-of-wedlock pregnancies, divorces, incarcerations, etc., to say nothing of fathers who neglect their family responsibilities—these things have increased more than ever before.

For many men and boys, including me, we know that deep down inside we *want* to be men. We know that we will *have* to be men. But if you knew the truth about men, you would realize that more than anything, we want to be sons. Therefore, we men must redeem ourselves to son-ship. We must stop waiting for our fathers to come to us; we must go to them to buy back from them our own son-ship. And this is entirely possible through a process I call "Redemptive Son-ship," a systemic method for both boys and men to get their son-ship from their biological fathers so that they are not trying to get it from every other relationship in their life. To do so, men need to acknowledge only one thing—"God was perfect in making me my father's son." We re-engage with our fathers from that perspective and we live through that reality.

Fathers are crucial in the lives of their children, especially their sons. Fathers have a great responsibility to care for and raise their children, but children also have the responsibility of obeying and respecting their father. The Bible lays it out this way:

For Parents:

> [4] "Hear, O Israel! The LORD is our God, the LORD is one! [5] You shall love the LORD your God with all your heart and with all your soul and with all your might. [6] These words, which I am commanding you today, shall be on your heart. [7] You shall teach them diligently to your sons and shall talk of them when you sit in your house and when you walk by the way and when you lie down and when you rise up. [8] You shall bind them as a sign on your hand and they shall be as frontals on your forehead. [9] You shall write them on the doorposts of your house and your gates.
> **(Deuteronomy 6:4-9)**

This is a reflection on the heart of God concerning commitment to families—especially, the relationship between children and their parents.

Here we get a glimpse of how much God expects us to be committed to Him. We can also see how desperate is His desire for generational blessings and commitment for His people. He's the Good Parent with children who learn from Him by instruction and experience, but He persuades them through teaching and commitment. God thinks in terms of family, not individualization. He's concerned with systemic and communal relationships and puts the responsibility on parents to ensure the children get that.

Other relevant scriptures: Proverbs 19:18, 22:6

For Mothers:

> ^{28} *Her children rise up and bless her;*
> *Her husband also, and he praises her, saying:*
> ^{29} *"Many daughters have done nobly,*
> *But you excel them all."*
> **(Proverbs 31:28-29)**

The response a woman gets from both her children and her husband is a reflection of her character. For this woman, her efforts are poured into both ends of her love life—both the children and her husband. She has an amazing way of nurturing her children while loving her husband. She doesn't seek to get her children to meet her emotional needs when she feels neglected by her husband, and she doesn't take her frustrations of caring for her children out on her husband. She's balanced and her entire house responds by blessing and praising her. For some women, the response of the children when they call her "blessed" is enough. But in truth, the blessing of the children is not enough without the praise of the husband and the praise of the husband is insufficient without the blessing of the children. Such a woman knows how to get both and she does so without complaining about it.

For Fathers:

> ^{4} *Fathers, do not provoke your children to anger, but bring them up in the discipline and instruction of the Lord.*
> **(Ephesians 6:4)**

7: The Importance of Being a Son

This is an imperative statement. It is clear and direct. It's a command, not an idea or suggestion. It also gives us the opportunity to understand that there can be significant distortions in the relationship between a father and his children with the possibility that the father can provoke a child to anger.

Anger seems to be produced somewhere between the tension of a father having authority and a son being subordinate to that authority. A hallmark of son-ship is subordination. But healthy subordination comes with great internal conflict. Feelings of discouragement, low self-esteem, depression and fear manifest as anger and unresolved anger prevents subordination and hinders properly executed authority.

Other scriptures: Colossians 3:21

Children:

> [8] *Hear, my son, your father's instruction*
> *And do not forsake your mother's teaching;*
> [9] *Indeed, they are a graceful wreath to your head*
> *And ornaments about your neck.*
> **(Proverbs 1:8-9)**

This passage expresses God's concern for children and how he empowers them to attend to Godly instruction. He doesn't want them to miss anything that's good for them. He gives them the map to Godly development as though just growing up, in and of itself, is not enough. He doesn't want them to simply grow up. He wants them to grow *in*: into themselves and a good understanding of who they are; into Him and how their relationship with Him impacts their life; into their family; into a relationship and into the world and how they fit in the big picture of God's plan for their life. So it's not just about getting big; it's more about growing from the inside out.

Other relevant scriptures: Proverbs 7:1-3

Even though it sometimes seems most of the world has given up on fatherhood (and maybe you are reading this book and have given up on your father, your children's father, or you know someone who has done so), I can't because I believe that God has always had a plan for children through their fathers. To reiterate this fact, let's look at another passage of scripture. It's one of my favorites: Malachi 4:6.

Theologically this passage is addressing the return of the lost (people) to God (their righteous father), on whom they had turned their backs. But I think, practically, it also speaks of God's heart for fathers and their children; that even though we see fathers dropping out of the game and children growing up hating and despising their fathers, there is still hope—especially in God. Because of all the things God could have addressed prior to closing His mouth for over 400 years,[9] He chose to talk about a return of children to their father.

> [6] *And he shall turn the heart of the fathers to the children, and the heart of the children to their fathers, lest I come and smite the earth with a curse.*
> **(Malachi 4:6 KJV)**

---

[9] There are no words recorded in Scripture, no prophetic messages from God to His people, no stories—He stopped talking until He spoke to the Virgin Mary though the angel Gabriel: [31] "And behold, you will conceive in your womb and bear a son, and you shall name Him Jesus." (Luke 1:31)

What a dynamic portrait! Doesn't it almost bring tears to your eyes as you envision children running to their fathers, sons restoring themselves to son-ship as they forgive and accept God's plan for their life?

Amazing! Son-ship being redeemed and everything the devil meant for evil being turned around to good. Despite all the negative things we hear and see, we should be mindful that there is a supernatural intervention taking place and it would be wise for us to get on board with God in this great work of Redemptive Son-ship.

Let me show you how this can come about for the man in your life. Maybe you're thinking, "Wow, I wish this could happen for my husband or my boy!" Maybe, you're even weeping because you've witnessed the disastrous effects of a toxic father/son relationship. Maybe you've noticed how it's hurting your man, but you never knew how to fix it. Or maybe, you're rethinking your own relationship with your father because you're starting to see it from a different perspective.

Whatever the insight; here's the plan:

BECOMING A SON:

In 2009, I began to work on the concept of Redemptive Son-ship from which much of what I talk about in this chapter is adopted.

In order to appropriately understand manhood you must understand boyhood, because life as a boy is ingrained in life as a man and healthy manhood is only attained once you have been a son. Not a momma's baby or a mother's little boy, but a father's son. Every boy deserves the right to be his father's son just by virtue of being born of his father's seed. It is one thing to be a boy; it is another to be a son. A mother can help her boy grow towards manhood by identifying the things in her that he needs to pushed away from and the things in his father he needs to be pushed towards.

A number of significant things happen between boyhood and manhood and son-ship is one of them. Son-ship is the affirmation process that boys go through which identifies and confirms them as men. This process involves both the boy's mother *and* father because it involves pushing and calling.

Boyhood is a developmental designation. Son-ship is an honorable standard. Son-ship represents the loving influence of a father and that a boy has knowledge of and is connected to his genetic bloodline. Boyhood only designates being born male. Son-ship means that he is born well. Son-ship gives insight into a boy's individual makeup—how he thinks, the opinions he holds, his paradigm.

Son-ship is that affirmation of existence a boy experiences when he sees himself as:

- an extension of his father;
- a reflection of his father and the humble discipline that entails; and
- being under the tutelage and leadership of his father.

When I refer to Redemptive Son-ship, I am using the term "redemptive" in both the Christian perspective of being redeemed—made free from the power of evil—and in the perspective of buying back, trading in or improving (as in "he redeemed himself by taking out the garbage").

7: The Importance of Being a Son

Boys have the power and ability to buy back what rightfully belongs to them: their son-ship. I don't believe a man can truthfully learn to love a woman until he has learned to love his father. And most men are missing—partially, if not completely—the component of being the sons of their fathers. They are Momma's boy but lack being Daddy's son. So Redemptive Son-ship is the process by which boys and men become the sons of their father. A boy's relationship to his father is obviously one of the most significant and necessary relationships in his life. It is precisely this relationship that many men lack and which I want to help them redeem.

When a boy learns that he is loved and protected by his father and, in exchange, accepts discipline and direction from his father, he is enjoying son-ship. Son-ship is that place where a boy, in his relationship with his father, finds confidence in being a boy; where everything about boyhood is o.k. His challenges are neutralized as he realizes through his relationship with his father that he is a son. Love, respect, mentoring, direction, hope, and faith are built into his character during this state of development.

Son-ship is the training ground for real life. At this stage, a boy learns to discipline his passions and lives to make his father proud. Eventually he will move from this state to independent manhood, where he will exchange the grace of this earthly son-ship for the reality of a heavenly son-ship—being under the direction of God, independent of his father.

To be a true son is one of the highest and most important pursuits to which any male can be called. I believe that every boy should have the opportunity to be a son before he becomes a man. Those who have experienced son-ship are more prone to develop into healthy men. Have you ever noticed how a boy who has a broken relationship with his father hates hearing that man call him "son?" Because "son" implies more than just coming from a man's seed; it implies that "you guided me and you led me to be a man even more than you loved me." Boys whose fathers have been absent in their lives despise being called son by their dads. It bothers them at the core of their being. These youngsters were never provided with the things needed for them to claim true son-ship.

Now let's talk about how son-ship is developed. (And I remind you that, as most boys are propelled to manhood, or at least a false sense of manhood, the development of son-ship has been entirely skipped over.) Redemptive Son-ship has several stages; each stage is designed to move the boy towards his father, which ultimately moves him towards son-ship.

There are five things that must happen for a man or boy to redeem his son-ship: exploration, reflection, forgiveness, restoration and celebration.

Exploration: A son must have as many opportunities as possible to talk about his father. He needs a chance to talk about the things he knows about his dad, the things he doesn't know and the things he has to guess at. Talk, talk, talk! His father may be the last thing a son wants to talk about if they are estranged, but it is also the most important because it is essential to his understanding of who he is. I call this stage of Redemptive Son-ship "Exploration" because at this point when you talk with your son (or husband) about his father, that's all you're doing together: exploring, thinking and talking. You will really appreciate this person more if you can get him talking about his father. It will also help you begin to understand what's in his heart.

Reflection: This part of the conversation goes a little deeper and discusses how a son feels about the things he knows about his dad. This is when men get in touch with their feelings, not just in general, but more specifically about their father. Here is where a man or boy hurts the most and where his heart begins to break, and also where the healing begins. If he can learn to feel for Dad, then he can also feel for his wife, children and everything else. Help him to go beyond the talking and get to his feelings. Get him to discuss more than just the fact that he's angry with Dad for not being around. Ask him where his anger lives inside him. Get him to describe it as if he were painting a picture of how it feels.

Resolution: The third thing a son needs is the opportunity to forgive. I say opportunity because, if his heart can't talk about and feel for his father, then he can never forgive. It's only after you are so close to pain that you can touch it and explain it that you can truly forgive. I call this stage "Resolution" because it systematically resolves everything by resolving the main thing. Men run on batteries and a son has to change up the battery that motivates his thinking and behavior. But forgiveness gives him the opportunity to remove the anger that is driving him to be better than or different from his father. Forgiveness lets the cross of Jesus be his new battery and lets what Christ did for him fuel his motivation in life and business. A man's worship has to shift from the idol of hatred and anger he has towards his father and life to one of the cross. He needs to crash at the cross and be propelled to love the man God chose as his father. Yes, that imperfect man, those imperfect situations and all the things a son might wish never happened *did* happen and God is using the son to confront them. In this stage, the forgiveness a son offers is not necessarily for his father's benefit, but more for his own. Because the son is the one who wants to love and to be in love. It is the son who wants to change the next generation. It is the son who is turning the corner towards a healthier and bigger tomorrow. So let it be the son who takes the first step to forgive and then let go of the outcome, over which he has no control.

Restoration: In this fourth stage, the emerging man grabs that little boy who lives inside him and walks him to his father in a different way. This is where the man takes the opportunity to do what the scared, hurt little boy would never do. This is the moment when he loves *himself* enough that he is able to talk to Dad at a graveyard, in a prison, on the phone, in a shelter, or wherever he can find him. This is the moment when everything in the son comes out and confesses that this man *is* his father. This is the moment he says, "I am my father's son."

Whether things were good, bad or unbelievably painful, it doesn't matter because at this moment the grown son is teaching the boy within himself to accept God's great gift of being created from his father's seed. This is the moment that gives him the courage to handle bold encounters productively for the rest of his life. This is when the son is born and the boy is affirmed. This is when a man's life is made real because there can be no true manhood where there has been no son-ship.

Celebration: When the one you love—your son or your partner—fully recognizes and acknowledges the truth that he is his father's son, it is a cause for celebration! You can help him reinforce this giant step in his life by revisiting the issue with him and celebrating that truth. There are prodigal sons, but there also prodigal fathers and *his* father has been returned to a rightful place in his son's heart. Even if circumstances prevent his dad being physically present and involved, what has occurred on the inside—the spiritual evolution—is as important as an actual birthday. Treat it that way!

If you, as wife or mother, can help to buy this person back to son-ship, you may change his life forever. Between boyhood and manhood lies son-ship and without son-ship it is impossible for any boy to truly become the real, self-actualized man he needs and *wants* to be for the people he cares about.

> *²⁶ For you are all sons of God through faith in Christ Jesus.*
> **(Galatians 3:26)**

8

A MAN'S FEAR AND ANGER

Anger is a problem for men. But if men are to be soldiers for their life, family and communities, then they need to get comfortable with expressing it. But how can a man make anger work for him in his life so that it doesn't damage all his relationships? As men mature, they must begin to understand the dynamics of anger and the underlying issue of fear.

LIFE IS TOUGH; DEAL WITH IT!

When men learn this lesson, they graduate from the lower school of deceit, excuses and illogical reasoning to the University of Manhood. Most men are not ready to face the reality that life is tough. That's why so many of our boys are found not just dropping out of school, but in juvenile institutions, jail and penitentiaries. Many of them give up on the ideals of hard work, delayed gratification, relentless moral living and personal commitment. They quit school because it takes too long; they quit work because they are undisciplined; they quit their families because they fear accountability and responsibility.

But they can't quit anymore!

In this chapter I want to call men back to the reality that "Life is tough; deal with it!"

It used to be normal for our elders to tell us that life was hard and we had to make the best of it. But those elders are gone and now too many parents, caregivers, mentors and other adults want to "save" our boys from the difficulties of life. In the process of protecting our children, we become enablers. We don't let them tread water long enough to see they really can swim. We don't give them the chance to fail anymore. Maybe it's because we're afraid they might not make it or maybe it's because only one side of the sword is sharpening the majority of our boys. That feminine influence has cut so deep to one side that it's weakening boys. We've got to find a way to cut from the other side.

One of the scariest moments of my life was when I had to jump into 10 feet of water during my military training. As I stood on the platform and watched the boys ahead of me jump in, I began to think about how scared I really was. I had never been in a pool before. I didn't know how to swim and I was so far away from my momma that I couldn't yell for her. I thought the higher-ups should have walked us into the pool rather than making us jump in. I thought they should have held our hand and progressively let us learn to let go. But they were not interested in being my mother. They were cutting the umbilical cord and bringing me to independence in a single step—literally.

Three boys went ahead of me and after each jumped in, my heart pounded as though it was going to spring right out of my chest. When it was time for the guy right in front of me to take the plunge, he began to shake and say "No!" God, I started getting even more nervous. I began to think, "Now why you gotta be acting like that? Don't you know I have to jump next?" The fellow began to cry and, crying, he walked off the board and dropped into the pool. He didn't do it with courage or because of the command to jump; he walked off the board as if to say he was going to die.

Then it was my turn. One command to jump, two deep breaths and I leaped! As I was falling, it seemed like it took forever to get to the water, so I opened my eyes to see where I was. And that's when I hit the surface. But I discovered I was able to see under the water. So, o.k., now I'm in a place I had never been before and I'm actually looking at it. Yep, you probably guessed—I nearly passed out. But the air in my lungs carried me to the surface and guards pulled me out with a rope. Here's what I learned: I didn't have to swim, I just had to jump.

After that experience, my whole perspective of life began to change. I began to realize that life had nurtured me so far; it had enabled me to be good but not to be a man. The dynamics of fatherlessness began to ring in my head like loud bells. I knew something was wrong. I knew that I had missed something important and that I would spend the rest of my life trying to find it.

Sometimes men have to learn to jump in order to realize they don't have to swim. It's the jumping that God is looking for and, if they do that, God will do the rest. So the latter (swimming) was the fear, but the former (jumping) was the problem.

Fear paralyzes men and makes them see the ocean as one huge hole in the ground. Fear allows them to see only the surface and leaves what's underneath to the imagination. If you begin to wade in at the beach, you realize that the shore slopes gradually into the water. Unless you walked in, you would never know that. If you let it, fear can give you answers to questions you never asked—the *wrong* answers. It paints realities that you have never tested because fear knows that, once you do, you will know the truth. And when you know the truth, you will no longer be afraid. As Jesus said on the

Mount of Olives: "Then you will know the truth, and the truth will set you free." (James 8:32.)

IS IT ANGER OR IS IT FEAR?

Normally, a man who is afraid is also angry. He doesn't want to show his fear in public, so he trains himself to express fear as anger to make it "manly." The angrier he is, the more afraid he is.

But why is he so scared? Why is he so timid? Well, it's because he was never allowed to be fearful as a boy. He was never given the opportunity to show fear in public. Or, if he did, he was ridiculed or punished. So he had to lie and pretend that he had it all together. Or he retreated back to the safety of the world of women. His brain was well trained by the dynamics of his environment.

When men get scared, everybody gets scared. So men have had to wear masks that literally hid them from themselves, along with the rest of the world. If only you can help him take off the mask and move away from the village of women, he'll be free to join the men in the hunting fields. Then and only then will he rise up hunting on behalf of his family and stop hurting the ones he cares most about.

Most of what your man (or your growing son) fears is behind him, but he thinks it's in front of him. I have to remind men constantly that you cannot be afraid of what has already happened; fear is always for what's to come and never what's in the past. They keep looking back as though the greatest challenges are sneaking up behind them when, in fact, their greatest tests are ahead of them. If men keep fighting the shadows at their backs, they never have to face the things in front of them. There has to be a turning to the future. A man must turn and face forward to overcome his fears. If he's looking backwards, his fear will always catch him unprepared. He has to stop worrying about looking brave to other people, but rather feel afraid and go forward anyway. I was scared when I jumped, but I still jumped.

Men need to understand that the objective of fear is respect and reverence. Fear is a real thing that can lead you to the wrong thing. When bullies bully it is to get the respect of the victim. But "healthy" fear should also lead to respect. As long as you are scared of it, you will act right around it. If I am afraid of death, I am going to respect it. If I am afraid of snakes, I will show my respect and keep a healthy distance away.

On the other hand, men will disrespect what they are not afraid of. Until something happens to make them afraid of it, whatever it is they disrespect will never have significant influence in their life.

You can see how fear can literally control the minds of men. A man will have many opportunities to be afraid and everything he is afraid of gains power and control over his life. So when men feel fear, they should automatically begin investigating the object of their fear. Is it something they *should* have a healthy fear of, or are they just shadow boxing with a ghost of the past that no longer exists? This kind of insight will help them make fewer mistakes in the realm of spiritual warfare, so that they are not aimlessly swinging in the air and hitting nothing.

THE WARRIOR CONCEPT

"Be a soldier. Be a soldier. Hey soldier!"

These were my uncle's words to me at the beginning of a long conversation about life. In reflection, I think the only part I really understood was him calling me "soldier" to get my attention. After that I was pretty much lost. But if you think about it, calling me a soldier presupposed that I was made for battle. That life isn't just about living but about fighting, as though there were battles ahead of me I had not perceived and I was already involved in training I was not aware of. Experiences like this made me angry and when I became angry, I would feel out of control.

Remember, Godly manhood is about a guy's keeping his composure, not blowing his cool and repressing his emotions. So if he becomes angry, he's lost control. That's why men involved in domestic violence continue the cycle of abuse, even though they promise it will never happen again. They externalize their anger and this type of behavior often results in shame, which then compounds the anger. They feel out of control, so they become even angrier and use that anger to try to oppress their victims (usually a family member). Their anger makes them feel powerless, so they exert power over their victims to satisfy the dangerous dragon inside themselves that, in truth, feels so scared and so vulnerable.

A few years ago, Tyler Perry produced a movie about an angry black woman.[10] The title was intriguing; the content is even more interesting. Because, you see, when men refer to an angry black woman, it seems humorous because men don't usually think of women's anger as dangerous or controlling—or even as justified. If she's angry, then she's just "crazy," or a "nag." But basically she's harmless and the butt of guy jokes.

Historically, women have not been referenced as angry. However, the truth is to the contrary. As a matter of fact, I have spent countless hours counseling women and giving

---

[10] Tyler Perry, *Diary of a Mad Black Woman* (Lions Gate Entertainment, 2005)

them permission to let their anger out because most of the time it *is* justified. But that's a whole other book!

For men it's a different story. Men's emotions are restrictive. They have them; they are just restricted. One of the main reasons is because men are challenged by their own definition of masculinity. They feel they have to protect their masculinity by restricting their emotions. Controlling and hiding anger is one way they attempt to do this. Women don't have this challenge.

Anger is a man's familiar companion. They know anger well and in many cases society expects men to get angry. Still, it is hard for a man to own his anger. Most of it is externalized and he blames the end result of his anger on others. "I only bumped into her and she fell down." He doesn't see the correlation between the bumping and the falling. He might take responsibility for the bump but blames the result of the bump on the victim.

ANGER, ATTITUDE & ALTITUDE

Sometimes men get angry because something happened to them that they perceive as unfair. This anger begins to shape their attitude and gives them a victim mentality or the opposite attitude that someone owes them something. And either attitude can make them feel like their *altitude* is in jeopardy, that there are limits on how high they can go in the world.

Young men are taught that attitude determines altitude, but nothing could be further from the truth. Men must understand that attitude is one thing and altitude is another. Attitude has to do with feelings and the meaning you give those feelings. It also represents what men hold dear inside themselves—things like moral character, patience, love, gentleness, self-esteem.

Altitude has to do with the level or height of success a man can reach—the outward stuff like guts, grind, strategy, etc.

So attitude and altitude sit at opposite ends of the spectrum of life's aptitudes and to reach his maximum potential, a man needs both. Only by working from both ends will a man be able to remove the glass ceiling which is just a mindset caused by living at only one end of the spectrum.

Some men are respectful, moral, kind, gentle, patient and overall good Christians, but they are also lazy and unorganized. A man can be as Christian as he wants to be, but if he doesn't work relentlessly hard, have the guts to make hard decisions and build vision and strategy for himself, he will never accomplish his goal. He needs to understand he doesn't have to just look through the glass longingly at his dreams on the other side. He can break it! He just needs to get over his issues (being a victim; feeling like the world owes him). To reach the height of success, a man needs to bend down and humbly ask for forgiveness from God and then get to work chipping away at the glass in the name of Jesus. The only one who should be mad now is the devil!

MY MESSAGE TO MEN:

Stop standing against everybody and everything and stand up for yourself! Your anger is not scaring anyone. The roaring flames you fire from your impulsive and immature temper tantrums are not scaring anyone but yourself. They are scaring you away from getting to work on your own glass ceiling. The enemy knows that, once a man stops focusing on everyone else and stops blaming everyone else for his problems, he is destined to become all that God is calling him to be. So man up and stop bullying others because you don't have the guts to take responsibility for yourself! Once you stop being so fearful, your anger is going to melt away.

Life is tough; deal with it!

> [7] *For God has not given us a spirit of timidity, but of power and love and discipline.*
> **(Timothy 1:7)**

9

PRINCIPLES, PRIORITIES AND POWER

In his motivational books and seminars, the late Zig Ziglar often said, "It was character that got us out of bed, commitment that moved us into action and discipline that enabled us to follow through." Those three words—character, commitment and discipline—should fasten themselves to the heart of every man who really wants to make a difference in his life. Character is that platform from which all of his life is lived. Commitment is the psychosocial persuasion that glues him to his responsibilities. And discipline is the classroom that never lets him skip class.

I have lived by that quote for a very long time. Zig Ziglar wrote as though character has the ability to move us, discipline has the ability to keep us going and commitment is that middle trait that pulls character and discipline together. I'm not sure that was his intent, but that's what it has meant to me as I have wrestled with trying to understand what causes so many men to live without principles and priorities.

Did you ever wonder why most men are so uncommitted? Think of all the ones you have known; now think of their character and discipline. There is a high correlation between men who are uncommitted and men who lack discipline and character. Character and discipline are the two biggest indicators you can have that a man may eventually be committed to you. Some women look for commitment without first seeking evidence of character and discipline. It just doesn't happen that way. You need the former *and* the latter to have a commitment that glues the two together. In the same way, a man cannot have priorities where he has no principles because principles drive priorities. And without both principles and priorities he will be spinning his wheels looking for the next get-rich scheme, the next woman to have sex with or the next idea to ruminate about.

THE FOUR COMMITMENTS

To enter a state of true manhood, a man must make four major commitments that are driven by his principles. Commitment One and Commitment Two really go hand-in-hand, you can't have one without the other and so they occur pretty much simultaneously and are inextricably linked.

Commitment 1—Commitment to God

This commitment is closely married to Commitment Two, the commitment to self. When we engage in self-exploration we obviously begin within. But as we gain insight, we move naturally and instinctually away from self and towards God. When a man truly starts to get in touch with who he is, he begins to see how dependent he is on all that life has to offer. A wise man does not stop with self-actualization (to realize fully one's potential), but aspires to achieve self-realization (the act of achieving the full development of your abilities and talents). This commitment reminds him he is "not all that"—not as important as he thinks he is! Here he moves from thought to action (logic to locomotion) because he realizes he needs someone greater than himself, otherwise he will destroy himself. He needs God.

9: Principles, Priorities and Power

Commitment 2—Commitment to Self

Commitment to God is our primary, most essential, most imperative commitment. However, we do not come to that commitment before we have dealt with and explored our commitment to self. This commitment is really about personal responsibility; the way the man takes care of himself—i.e., he is responsible to his own person. Most men will dress nice, drive nice and dream nice, but deep inside they are broken. Commitment to the self allows a man the opportunity to put himself before everything else in his life in a healthy way. It helps him to grow and gain deep insight from his experiences and literally transforms and shapes his worldview.

Commitment 3—Commitment to Family

This commitment concerns the responsibility a man has for the people who are most important to him. This is the commitment I call the "circle in the circle." It is the tight-knit group within the big circle of the world. And this is what a true man feels it (life) is all about. Family is the core of his motivation and his life—an extension of the "self." This is the place he would die for. These are the people he would give everything up for. These are the ones who are more important to him than he is to himself, the relationships that give rise to the logical and emotional reasons why he chooses to live and work. This is the group that he feels it's all for—the group that's the hardest to make happy and the most difficult to leave.

A man should commit to his family even when he's not necessarily in agreement with all the things that may be going on. Family is everything. The aspirations and vision he has for life are all centered on and motivated by the family. This is the circle in the circle that knows him as a person and not just a personality. Every man needs this. It is so basic that, even if he isn't living within his own biological family, he should create a family from close friends or his church community. Groups are more powerful than individuals and a man will gain personal power through surrounding himself with caring individuals.

Commitment 4—Commitment to Life (Work and World)

This commitment is the one I call "the big circle." It includes components such as work, business, church and community. It broadens his perspective and gives a man a larger arena in which to feel and be responsible. It helps him figure out how he's connected to the bigger world. It presupposes that he was born for something greater than himself and his family. Although he should never put it first, the larger group is where most of the exchanges happen in his life. He interacts with it, respects it and reaps the benefit of his involvement in it. A man should not spend more time here than with the first three commitments, yet Commitment Four is where he's called to most frequently. This commitment also gives him the opportunity to participate in things bigger than he is, which helps to keep him balanced. Participating in the big circle keeps his ego in check so that he never gets to the point where he thinks of himself as the greatest thing that life has ever offered. In this commitment a man will always find people better than he is, as well as people not as good; it is here that he maintains his perspective as to who he is and who he could become. A man without this commitment is a man destined to feel anger, discouragement and depression.

What do The Four Commitments have to do with principles and priorities? Men make their commitments based on a logical set of underlying and guiding principles. I repeat, you can't have priorities without having principles because principles drive priorities. Biblical principles drive life priorities.

They help you to have an organized system of living (thoughts and actions). When principles are married to priorities, personal power is born. This is a power that every man needs but in many cases—because of the responsibility that comes with it—this is the power that most men avoid.

INTEGRITY, THE PRIMARY PRINCIPLE

A man has to live his life with a guiding set of principles. He has to make decisions about how he will love, how he will live and how he will die. If he wants to be recognized for anything, he should strive to be recognized for his integrity. The driving principle in his life should be his own individualized integrity. Living by the principle of integrity should be his top priority. From there he must establish other principles that will both maintain that integrity and define how he will live and how he will love in integrity.

"What is the most important thing in this world to me and what will I do about it?" Every man should ask himself this question at some point in his life. Most men put everything before their own integrity. They will mention their family, their church, God, their wife, their business, but very rarely will they mention their integrity. That's because they don't start with the least common denominator, themselves. As a result, they find that everything they prioritize suffers because they didn't make integrity their first priority.

One evening I was explaining to a group of men what integrity is and how it operates. Several guys in the room that day were far from living a life of integrity. Even the ones who were didn't seem to have a clear idea of what the word means and what it was they were doing that defined them as men of integrity. They had heard the word. They knew that it had something to do with character, but none of them could actually come up with a definition of integrity.

Well, here's your take away: Integrity is that moral and logical system learned from another so intimately that the system becomes your own. According to the Cambridge Dictionary of American English (online edition),[11] integrity is "the quality of being honest and having strong moral principles." It comes from the Latin *integritatem* meaning "soundness, wholeness, blamelessness," which in turn comes from *integer*, which means "whole" or "incorrupt." The only way for a person to have true integrity is to take time to define his personal values and then to draw a line in the sand, so to speak, that he or she refuses to cross, even when no one else is looking.

When a man *integrates* his life, thinking, behavior and principles with God, he gains integrity. Integrity doesn't begin with you, but it does end with you. Thus, the best way you can encourage the man or boy in your life to live honestly and truthfully, is for you yourself to live in integrity. Do what you say you will do. Don't make promises you don't intend to keep. Be firm with your children and honest with your spouse. When it comes to the hard decisions, pray for guidance and then bite the bullet and do what you know is right!

You can also acknowledge when your husband (or son) is right in order to encourage his movement towards integrity. Men love to be right, even if they do wrong. The more you acknowledge the moments in your relationship where he *is* right and honestly and genuinely encourage that, the more he will want to *do* right.

Integrity has to begin with principals outside yourself and then be integrated with your personality. It's not just about adopting

---

[11] http://dictionary.cambridge.org/dictionary/american-english

9: Principles, Priorities and Power

principles; it is actually *becoming* those principles. It is not a thought, an idea or a feeling. Applying integrity to a system of principles born of deep and passionate convictions can make them, through logic and reasoning, a concrete roadmap to all good things.

When men make integrity a priority in life, they make faithfulness their life goal—not just faithfulness to the woman in their life, but to total right living. While their integrity influences their marriages and families in very powerful ways, they also influence politics, neighborhoods, the young and, more importantly, it pleases God. Many ask if true integrity is even possible. Not only is it possible, I believe it's necessary.

Why has it become common practice in America and across the world for great men to fall into sexual misconduct, so much so that people have begun making excuses for them? It's almost as though citizens believe men are just vulnerable creatures by nature, weak when placed in the hands of sexual temptation and destined to succumb to sexual seduction—"they can't help it, they're made that way!"

As much as you love them; as much as you would give everything for them to love you the way you love them; as much as you hoped you would be the only one they give themselves to, the reality is that love alone is just simply not enough to keep a man faithful. Take the story of David in the Bible, for example.

David was a man after God's own heart, but David slept with a married woman, whose husband, Uriah, respected him as a leader. He sent Uriah into battle, knowing that he would be killed. Uriah willingly gave his life to die under David's leadership (Samuel 2:11). I think that, although we've preached David's sin into the ground, we've missed the same thing David missed. What was God trying to teach through Uriah? What was God showing us in the contrast between these two men? David loved God, but that wasn't enough to keep him from doing wrong because love alone is not strong enough to prevent wrongdoing. What Uriah had, David needed but couldn't see. Uriah had *integrity*. And unless *you* get it, you—just like David—will forever be vulnerable to harming the people you say you love.

There doesn't need to be a problem in a relationship for someone to cheat. Cheaters don't cheat because they don't love their partner. In fact the problem is never with love and it is normally not with the person who was cheated on. The problem is with the cheater. You can actually love someone very deeply and still cheat on them (David loved God deeply). I wish the statement, "If you really loved me, you wouldn't have cheated on me," were true, but it simply is not. A man's cheating has less to do with you and how much he loves you and more to do with the fact that he doesn't love or respect himself enough to not cheat. And until cheaters see in themselves what David failed to see in Uriah, they will never be able to be faithful. It's lack of integrity that's the problem. If he's cheating, it's not you that is broken, *he is*!

Integrity is the only thing that really prevents cheating. People with integrity don't cheat because their integrity doesn't allow it. They are faithful when they date and they are faithful when they marry because something has happened in their heart— and it has also happened in their head. When love ties the head and heart together, integrity is born. And this integrity keeps a man consciously "on camera" even when there's no camera in sight. This is not just personal discipline. This is a change of heart. "Therefore, my dear friends, as you have always obeyed—*not only in my presence, but now much more in my absence*—continue to work out your salvation with fear and trembling..." (Philippians 2:12)

LIVING WITHOUT LIMITS

It is commonly said that what goes up must come down and most men have actually bought into that concept. The fear of failure will very often cause a man to fall. When they reach certain levels of success, they begin to think of what the bottom will feel like. When things are going well for them, they begin worrying about what it will be like when things turn the other way. Sometimes apparently successful men are so consumed with the prospect of walking through the valley while they are actually still high on the mountain that they begin subconsciously to do things that cause them to fall.

How can we help men realize that what goes up doesn't have to come down? It's all about how high they go. If the rock is thrown high enough, it will escape Earth's gravity; it won't come down but, rather, will float in outer space. So remind him, "Stop fearing failure when God sprinkles success in your life and thrusts you even higher. Because the higher you go, the more unlikely it is that you will fall."

NO EASY WAY OUT

When men become discouraged or they begin to feel that their life is not where it should be, they begin to detach from their support team. They begin to isolate themselves or they run towards new people. Often their preference is for this new person to be a female or maybe a companion who will give them the feeling of a brand new start. Men love a new beginning; even if it's not really new, they like it if it *feels* new. The grass always looks greener on the other side of the fence. And sometimes it *is* greener—sometimes it is more beautiful, more manicured and much healthier.

But there's just one problem with the green grass on the other side. It's not his! He didn't work it. He didn't plant it. He didn't care for it. It's greener because it was taken care of, while the grass on his side is dying because he didn't cultivate it. Instead of trying to jump over to somebody else's lawn, that guy should grab his own water hose and begin watering his own grass. In the same way, he needs to do the work it takes in his relationships to keep them green and stop trying to live off the hard work of other people. Men need to let their integrity guide them through planting, watering and nurturing their own relationships and families instead of giving up so quickly. It's what's inside the man that makes this happen. Because at the end of the day the things on the outside may get him to the top, but it's what's on the inside that keeps him there.

KEYS & DOORS

There is nothing like having a key to the car you want to drive or the door of a room you need to get into. Keys give you access and it's always easier to get in with keys than to break in. When I was a youngster, I didn't have a set of keys to our home. My mother was usually in the house when I got back from school, but not always. I tried waiting for her, but it was very hot outside and my patience would sort of run out. So I would try to get in through a window. That was hard—I would have rather had a key.

Life provides new opportunities all the time. Some will simply come by luck—by being in the right place at the right time. Others by well thought-out strategy and doing the things that are necessary to get into certain places or to make certain things happen in your life. When men play around, chase women and live without focus, they become limited in their ability to open certain doors of opportunity. There are so many men who don't have keys—or have recklessly thrown away the keys they need to the doors they want to open. They may have a job, a home, a dream, but they simply don't have keys necessary to take advantage of new opportunities.

A man must also keep in mind that certain keys open only certain doors and a key that worked for one door may not work for all doors. So, he needs to get the specific keys to the specific doors he wants to open. In other words, he must prepare for every level of revelation that appears in his life. Everything that God plans has a key to it, because God's promises require the keys to Godly living—keys that allow a man to make life go the way of his dreams.

Therefore, a man must ask himself: "What door or doors do I need open in my life? Where and how do I get the key to unlock that door?" He should do this for everything he plans for and, doing so, he will bless both himself and the people who love him. Keys are power. They represent authority and ownership. The more keys a man has, the more power he has.

I once visited a small town where I was scheduled to speak at a business luncheon. The first thing the person who picked me up said to me was, "The mayor has given you the keys to the city."

I thought for a second: "Wow! What does that mean? What do I do with them? What do I ask for?" If I could wish for anything that this city had the potential to offer at this moment in my life, what would it be?

Now remember, I'm thinking I have the keys but I want to make sure that I maximize the opportunity that it offers me. I could have said, "Oh thanks but I'm fine." I could have played Mr. Humble and just let the opportunity pass me by. But I felt that God had given me the keys so that I could have a greater impact on my audience than I had planned and it was up to me to do the best thing.

With that in mind, I said to my host, "I want you to connect me with some of the most influential and powerful people in the state. I want the opportunity to turn poverty around by impacting the people directly. I want to teach on the concept of "Keys and Doors.' I want to unbreak broken hearts. And I want to do it quickly. I can have a bigger and more effective impact than all of your long-term grants and other government programs."

After I said that, I was like, "Wow! That was a lot to put out there." That was *big* for a small town. But when you take advantage of opportunities, regardless of how big or how small they are, you win.

When big dreamers walk into small places—when they perceive open doors and actually go through them to maximize the opportunity they present—they are intrinsically honoring God for giving them that opportunity. Then they leave it up to God to expand the grace of the open door. I walked away from that speaking engagement knowing that I had a key. I also knew that the pains of poverty and crime had prompted me to dream big in a small place. Although I only had an opportunity to speak in that particular place, God was giving me keys to other places because of what I desired when he gave me the keys to the city, including the opportunity to run a private Christian school for inner-city boys, the opportunity to start a community-based organization to treat mental health patients, an organization that helped transform the lives of juvenile delinquents and so much more.

I later thought to myself and was reminded by God that I was being given keys throughout my life: as I helped my mother, my family and others when I was young; as I refused to sell

9: Principles, Priorities and Power

drugs (and once bought drugs, not to use, but because I had the naive idea that, if I bought the drugs, my friend's addicted mother would not be able to). After dropping out of high school I went on to pursue dual masters degrees and multi-state licenses in mental health while at the same time after washing a car, turning that one wash into a full-fledged mobile detailing company; after cleaning a dental office, turning that into a janitorial company with over 50 employees; and after marrying my wife, raising our three children.

Yes, I did all that at the same time! But I am not trying to puff myself up in your eyes, dear reader. My point is that life is about keys and doors, about the faithfulness a man shows towards life and society, the hard work and determination he is willing put forth even through all his failures and the strength he is willing to show over and over again—this is what sets him up for success.

It's not always about how many doors are opened for a man during his life; it's really about how many keys he is given—keys that fit the locks and *could* open the doors of opportunity if he chooses to use them.

Some keys he may never use. Some keys will be passed along for use by the generations that come after him. And some keys will be for him. It's absolutely amazing to realize how many keys you may acquire in your lifetime. I envision being like the janitor with a ton of keys on my waist. I went after the degree; I went after the certification, I went after the licenses. Even if I never used a particular key, I knew I had it, and that empowered me.

What young men need to realize today is that their life doesn't necessarily have to be about getting rich at 16. It has to be about getting keys.

The keys should match the personality of the young man. Not everyone needs a college education although, if attainable, a college education is definitely a powerful key. Young men need to examine their life and be pushed towards a vocation. Many kids are, instead, drawn towards fame and money as ends in and of themselves. If they use the keys that open those doors, they think they are "mature"—the man. What they really need is to be pushed to use the keys that will open doors to the things that will leave them feeling they have made a contribution to the world. When they do that, the money and fame will follow—if that's also what they want.

Every parent should identify at least six keys they want their children to obtain by the 12th grade and another six keys by the age of 21. Because the world changes, the doors move, the opportunities rotate—you have to diversify the key set so that opportunity is at hand regardless of how long roads and dead ends may play out in your child's life.

The keys to opportunity have been available to me my whole life, just as they are to everyone—including your own son and partner. Men need to understand that there are some keys in life they were born with and there are some keys in life they will get as a result of relationships with other people.

Men need to be bold enough to go after those keys.

Men need to be bold enough to *win*!

> [33] *But seek first His kingdom and His righteousness, and all these things will be added to you.*
> **(Matthew 6:33)**

10

THE POWER OF PERSPECTIVE

A man who believes in God sets his heart to resolve the challenges of life that cannot be handled by his own strength alone. Everything about being a man has to do with strength. In fact, when you are an adolescent boy, not being athletic is definitely not cool because muscles and athleticism are so tied to manliness in our society. That's why so many young men who may not be athletes find themselves displaying their strength (manliness) through thug-like behavior and appearance. They perceive being a thug (strong) as an acceptable alternative and *way* better than being labeled a wimp.

Men are greatly challenged by the element of strength because it is easy to come by, yet very difficult to maintain. Each level of life brings a new level of strength leading to manhood and with that strength come new levels of responsibility. Everyone expects men to be strong. Even resilient, empowered women want men who can give direction, who have vision, who can rescue them from the dangers of the day and who can claim heroism as boldly as Superman, himself.

I'll never forget how my perception of my wife's gaze started changing as I began to understand the qualities of manhood. Initially, as she gazed into my eyes, I felt as though she was looking into my soul. Literally, that she had fallen so deeply in love with me that she would be lost without me. God, did that make me feel like a man! Later, that same look began to transform into words that softly whispered of things I never imagined could be expected of me. Her eyes were simply saying, "Take me somewhere, please." I could tell she wanted me to do more than love her. She wanted me to lead her. To make sure that her time with me is worthwhile. To make sure that the direction of her life could fit into the direction I was headed. That I wanted what she wanted—and she wanted all that life would offer us both. The shift was from a glance of romance to a glance of responsibility and that changed the game.

A woman wants her man to lead her into the unbelievable. She wants his love for her to redeem everything she was deprived of earlier in her life. She expects that giving herself to him for the rest of her life will buy back for her everything she had thought was lost. Women want to be loved at the deepest level and led to the highest level. She not only wants to *believe with* her partner, she also wants to be able to *believe in* her partner. She wants to know that being with him will make her safe. She wants to be able to help him when life gets tough and to hide behind him when life gets scary.

When my wife looked at me, I saw beyond the color of her eyes. I saw a young woman screaming for me. A woman who wanted more than anything to be able to lean and depend on a man she could trust. It wasn't about God this time or any aspect of religion. It was human, very human. It made me feel like I had gotten myself into something that I would never be able to shake off. Something in her look let me see not only the man I was at that moment, but beyond to the man I needed to be for her. I could feel her pain, sense her wounds and empathize with her fears. In the flash of a look, we became more than just good friends—now I was her man and she was my woman.

10: The Power of Perspective

Yet, with that wonderful step into the future came the painful and—yes, I can be honest—scary responsibility of taking her with me into our destiny. That was it. That's the something I felt: the need to take her to our destiny. Not just my destiny or her destiny, but *our* destiny. With that responsibility came the willingness to commit to a plan that would lead inexorably to unprecedented victories together. At that moment, I made a decision to love even when it got hard and to love even when the butterflies had flown away.[12] Henceforth, the world would know that we were—and still are—ride-or-die lovers. If either one of us were to go down, we both would fall. If she hurt, I hurt and if she became unhappy, then I would be unhappy, too.

My wife grew up without her biological father, so I knew that part of my responsibility was to buy that back for her—to give to her and treat her in a way that the losses she felt not having the presence and guidance of her biological father would be bought back.[13] She would never again be desolated by feelings associated with not having him around during her childhood. The things she should or could have learned from him would be taught through our relationship and the things she needed from him emotionally would be met in our relationship.

I realized that this thing was not all about me, but more about her. What she wanted and where she wanted to go. I would somehow answer the questions her eyes were asking. Where will we go? Where will you take me? I knew I had to do something to ensure that she could see the bright future I wanted to show her and could believe in what I saw for the both of us.

---

[12] You can learn more of what I mean about the "butterflies" by reading *Love Notes* (Leroy Scott Ministries, 2010).
[13] A form of redemption, which we will discuss at length in Chapter 15—Saving Our Sons.

In 2005, we planned our wedding together. We didn't have a lot of money but, God, did we have a lot of heart! We were young and brave; desperate for the best. So we traveled to New Orleans for a traditional French-style wedding. It was held outside and my bride rode up to the carpet on a carriage pulled by a white horse. I'll never forget it. She was beautiful, but I remember the *feeling* of beauty was resonating for me more than her actual physical beauty. It was beyond feeling great. I felt so responsible for her. I felt *so* responsible... I felt my new wife needed to win and that I had the privilege of setting up the game and the court she would win in.

In order to gain strength, I had to learn to lose strength. In order to lead, I had to learn to follow. In order be responsible, I had to be redeemed. In order to love, I had to be unconditionally loved. In order to be a man, I had to have a perfect model. In order to realize manhood, I needed a miracle.

So that "somewhere" is not necessarily an external, physical place. It is more an internal space: that space that holds the two of you together; that space that becomes a light in the dark times and a map of directions for confused moments.

Love is crazy-powerful and when a man realizes the responsibility he has to be a good steward of his marriage relationship, he has the power to make a great life for all the ones he loves.

The miracle of giving yourself away to God as if you were incapable of undertaking life on your own is far from what men seem designed to do. Yet, it is a necessary step if they are to become who they are meant to be. The things men do naturally and believe identify them as men were the very things I had to give up in order to gain true leadership. The definition of "up" was to go "down;" the definition of

10: The Power of Perspective

"strength" was to be "weak" and those ideals appeared far from what society normally sees as being a "man."

When men do this, they set themselves on a course not tied to the frustrations of their past, but rather to the fruition of their future. Their motives are driven by faith and the secrets of their hearts are healed without being revealed. They lead everything in one direction, making all things work together for the good of their family. When husbands believe God, the game changes.

Men need to give meaning to their life. It's not just the things they've been through in their life that are important, but rather what meaning those events have now that really matters. Ask yourself what the most difficult thing in your life meant to you? You will find that it's not the incident that is most difficult to deal with, but rather the meaning you gave the incident. As events happen in our life, the conscious mind has to do something with those events. One thing the psyche attempts to do in order to protect itself from traumatic past events is to interpret the event by making it meaningful.

In my book *Unbreaking the Heart*, I use the concept of Mental Interpretation to help people forgive. This is a very important—probably critical—because, if the interpretation of an event is wrong or if the interpretation causes someone to live in a dysfunctional way, then he or she is going to have serious problems in life. Because the unconscious is always trying to break through to consciousness, the suppressed interpretation of an event will play itself out in other areas of the person's life and they won't even realize it.

The good thing is that you can actually make events mean anything you want them to mean. You can reconstruct the meaning that your brain chose unconsciously and give it another meaning that promotes your ambition and success.

If a man whose father was not there for him perceives that to mean his father didn't love him, then he is going to be listening very intensely for conversations and themes to support that. If he thinks his father not being there means that his father was irresponsible and immature, then he is going to listen for those themes. The fact is, we look for and listen for the psychological meanings our brains have already given to incidents. So, what is your man telling himself about incidents that happened in his life? What meaning has he given things? And what can you do to help him correct those perspectives?

A man can only see what he's looking for by what he's looking through. That's right—it's all about the glasses he's looking through. It's all about how he filters things psychologically that determines what he sees. Most men evade these psychological truths out of fear of the suggestion that they have some kind of mental disorder. What they need to understand is that everyone is a little "mental;" it doesn't become a mental disorder until it adversely affects your ability to adapt normally, adjust and interact appropriately with your environment. It's like everything else in life—it's not a problem until it's a problem. And when it is a problem, that's when it needs to be dealt with. At least that's how most men see it.

I suggest that it's better to deal with an issue before it becomes a problem, so that it never has a chance to turn into a crisis. It is better to be preventive than to be reactive, but understanding the "why" is a matter of perception. Think about it for a second—it's better to disclose information that may hurt someone before they find out rather than waiting for them to learn about it from some other source. Imagine if a husband cheated on his wife but then was honest and told her about it immediately, rather than waiting for her to find out after he's in so deep it probably would end the marriage. Confession is a great tool, but only if the one confessing has an honest perspective.

Being reactive is waiting for the wronged one to find out before owning up to the indiscretion. Being preventative is confessing before they find out. Most people have a perception that love is somehow not powerful enough to cover wrong the right way, protecting and saving what they thought sin and hurt would break apart. So they often wait to be found out rather than getting in front of an issue and controlling it from the perspective of honesty. On the other hand, people with the perspective that love can pardon a multitude of sins and that it is better to tell the truth in love than to play games tend to focus more on their relationship with God and how that plays out in their responsibility to the ones they love. Most people say they would never tell their spouse when they have cheated because they know what the result would be. One guy actually told me only a fool would do that. But I always say that it is easier to be honest and live with yourself than it is to lie and live with the one you to whom you are telling lies.

"Oh what a tangled web we weave, when first we practice to deceive!"[14]

Jeffrey's Story

Jeff called me one day frantically wanting to discuss a dilemma regarding his relationship with his wife. He seemed very nervous as he told me the story and I imagined that he had not told anyone else about his situation. He said that he was so hurt by his mistake and needed to find a way out of his

---

[14] Sir Walter Scott, *Marmion*, Canto vi. Stanza 17.

predicament. He sounded pitifully sorry over the phone. I immediately knew I was dealing with a man who was guilty and repentant over his mistake. He said he hated himself for what he had done and rambled on about turning back the hands of time and having a second chance. All of this, before he actually got to his story.

Jeff was a 27-year-old professional financial investor. He was known for his integrity, hard work and determination. Everybody he knew looked up to him for his honesty, success and just all-around positive personality. Jeff had been married for five years. He and his wife had a wonderful relationship and Jeff loved her very much. He repeatedly mentioned how he would do anything for her. Well, one day Jeff was approached by a young lady who became very interested in him. Initially the relationship was a casual one, primarily focused on business. But gradually Jeff realized he was falling for the woman when he realized how excited he was to listen to her speak and hear her ideas. He found himself getting ready ahead of time for her—neatening the office, making sure his tie was straight and his voice was clear. He had even begun to position his degrees and accomplishments in a way that she would be sure to see them. Well, while he was falling, she was also falling. The problem was that she had nothing to fall from. She was a single, childless woman, while Jeff was a married man with two children.

One of the most painful and alarming memories Jeff related to me was actually making love to his wife while thinking about the other woman. He mentioned that this made him very scared. He didn't want to mess up. He didn't want to fall, but it was too late! Everything inside him had slipped into adultery. He eventually slept with the woman, telling himself that it was nothing more than sex. But he was so hurt by what he had done, that he cut the relationship off and told the woman he never wanted to

10: The Power of Perspective

speak with her again. She said she was fine with it; she told him that it was a mistake and they should both walk away from it.

Twelve months went by and Jeff struggled the whole year with what he had done. The biggest problem Jeff had would not seem like a problem to most men: he had cheated and his wife knew nothing about it. When he called me, he mentioned that he wanted to be honest with his wife because he loved her so much. Imagine that: after a whole year, you want to tell your wife you slept with another woman. What would you do? How would you handle that? Would you say he was crazy for doing such a thing? Or would you agree that he should tell her. My advice to Jeff was to do what he felt would help to relieve his shame so that he could live guilt free, whether that meant staying with his wife or living alone.

So Jeff did that and, although they struggled for the next six months, their marriage has become one of the strongest I've ever worked with.

You see, most couples want trust in their relationship, but don't really realize that you can't have trust until you have truth. Truth is a prerequisite to trust and if you want a real, loving, authentic relationship, you have to tell the truth in all situations. When I suggested to Jeff that he tell his wife the truth, I knew that God honors truth in relationships and, if you do what God honors, He will respond by blessing it. That didn't mean Jeff would not lose his family; it simply meant that Jeff would know in his heart that he had told the truth, rather than try to hide behind a mask that could have been torn off by someone else at any time.

When a man avidly seeks the true meaning around all the situations of his life, such as why is he engaging in things he knows he shouldn't or what motivates his anger or frustrations, he begins to approach life in a different way. When he grows enough to change his perspective, he begins asking hard questions, confronting people and holding himself and others accountable. He begins making decisions that exemplify his bravery. He begins to live his life as a real man rather than hiding from difficult things like a little boy. He begins to tell the truth to people he loves and cares about.

> *[23] Taking the blind man by the hand, He brought him out of the village; and after spitting on his eyes and laying His hands on him, He asked him, "Do you see anything?"*
> **(Mark 8:23)**

11

WHEN MEN FAIL

When men fail, they hurt. They hurt badly. They bleed on the inside. Yet somehow, somewhere along the way, they learn to bandage up the damage so that the world never knows their pain. When they cry, they cry in the corner, out of sight of the rest of the world.

Failing is embarrassing for a man. It makes him feel like he should have never even tried. It also enforces the idea that he should never try again. One attempt that fails is like an eternity. Most men would rather not try than try and fail. Men hate failure. But more than that, not only do they hate it—they are also afraid of it. So in essence they hate what they are afraid of and the fear keeps them from taking it straight on and dealing with it. They deny the fear and pretend that they can conquer things alone without anyone's help. Consequently, they miss out on having a man, father, coach or mentor in their life. Yet, men need to understand that every man needs at least one other man in his life; someone who can stand on the outside of his life looking in; someone who holds him accountable and responsible. Your man needs another man (or maybe two or three) to do the very things which fathers are called to do: guide, mentor, push, encourage and act as a sounding board to bounce his expanding ideas against. If he enjoyed this kind of father or father figure when he is young, so much the better. If not, help him to find these appropriate role models. Be careful when you suggest it, because he might get upset or offended. So do it gracefully.

When it comes to intimate relationships, most men would rather not commit in the first place than make a commitment and not keep it. Too many men give up on their families because their attempts to be a real part of the family have failed. This fear of failure is why it's so easy for a woman to chase a man away. He just gives up and throws in the towel instead of manning up and demonstrating that he can be a dependable, responsible partner.

Wilbert's Story

Wilbert thought he would be able to accomplish every dream he ever reached for. He was a college graduate with a promising career. He was a Christian and often helped other men find their purpose in life and reach their life goals. He came to see me because he was "tired." That is exactly what he said when I asked him how I could help him. Tired was the way he described his experience. I assumed that what he was trying to explain was how his outsides were catching up with his insides. How what he did for a living was now overwhelming how he actually lived.

During his first session, Wilbert began crying almost immediately—within five minutes of starting to tell me his story. He then took a deep breath and laid his head on the back of the couch as though he was far away from his experience. I didn't know exactly what the experience was and I didn't feel I needed to know. I could help him without the details. But Wilbert was adamant; he wanted me to hear his story as though just telling it to another person would help him. Emotionally insistent, he was trying to get to the story—or at least to the emotional place from where he could tell the story.

11: When Men Fail

I diverted him back to the present, asking him, "Wilbert, what do your tears mean? What are they saying?"

He replied, "I'm tired, so tired."

"Tired of what, Wilbert? What are they tired of?" (I strategically and metaphorically personified his tears, making it easier for him to talk about them and see himself as separate from them.)

"They are tired of trying so hard," he said, "So hard at being successful, helping people, pleasing people." Then he paused, put his hands over his head and said, "Oh God, they are tired of being a man."

I understood what he was saying and every man who reads this knows exactly what he meant. I reached for the alternative and asked, "Do they have another option? What do they want to be?" Without hesitation he said, "*A son!* I want to be held by a man. Yep, there is something in me that wants to hear the heartbeat of man. My wife's breasts are not working for this pain. As much as I have going for me, I feel like a failure."

Even after some discussion, Wilbert could not specifically put his hand on one thing at which he had failed at. Ultimately, his feeling of failure was not the reflection of his reality. It wasn't evident on the outside. It was all on the inside. He wanted to be a son. He wanted to be held by a man. Most fathers, or even other men, would have given him a big hug. That would have healed him on the outside. It would have pointed him towards the man who hugged him as a surrogate father figure. But it would have not healed the inside.

Wilbert needed something to point him to the inside—not to another man, but to the man he already was. So he hugged *himself* saying, "God I've come so far!" He laughed and added, "I'm crying all over your office."

You see sometimes you have to encourage yourself in the Lord. Sometimes, even if you do have mentors, you have to resist being rescued and fill that empty space on your own. Part of growing up, for a man, is becoming able to point his pain toward himself and find comfort there. When a little boy fails, he wants to just quit and blame someone else. But when Godly men fail, they take an honest look at their pain, own up to their responsibility for it, and move forward knowing that, with God's help, success could be just around the corner.

So what should your role be in all this? Keeping your man accountable can change both your life and his. Help him to hold up the mirror of honest perception and look deep within. Society had so shaped Wilbert's belief that he thought he had to cry alone in the dark. He developed illogical and irresponsible ways to resolve his perceived failures that didn't really work.

HITTING BOTTOM

The most painful falls a man takes are the ones where he feels like he'll never get on his feet again. They fall from such a height and they fall so hard that they just can't get back up. If they're lucky, they may be able lift themselves into a sitting position where they fell, but getting all the way up isn't going to happen. When they realize this, they wallow in the depression and disgust of what they have brought on themselves. Then they live with the regret of messing up or they attempt to change things, but they just can't get back to where they were.

Real men who fall this hard learn to sit up and do the best they can where they are sitting. They make the best out of their life. They build a perspective around their situation that allows them to continue to live out the promises of God in the state to which they have fallen.

God rewards this kind of man. When the entire world has turned its back on him because of his mistake and what he did is an embarrassment to him and those who believed in him, he settles down to work and just keeps on going.

That's why men need God's help. The mark of a true leader is realizing that humbling himself enough to reach out to God is a sign of strength, not weakness. Not asking for help just to make money and pay bills, but also appealing to God to keep him honest, humble and repentant. A man with a repentant heart handles failure much better than a man who hangs on to false pride and resentment, blaming others for his failure.

In all fairness I must say that sometimes men fail because of their own faults and other times they fail because of the faults of other people in their life. Sometimes it's the friends they choose to hang out with and, unfortunately, sometimes it's the women they choose to share their life with. A man and a woman have to be on the same page on the important things in their life. They may disagree on the details, but they have to agree on the long-term destiny. They have to focus more on the promise than they do the personality. Learning to get back to the reason God brought them together, rather than the little arguments and disagreements they'll have along the way, is like medicine to their relationship. If they don't do this, they will always pull each other down, both losing what they worked so hard to gain. So men have to make hard choices about who will be in their life and who has to leave their life and a man who can't do that will always set himself up for failure.

Men make choices that hinder their ability to live out what God has intended and planned for their life. Some men make the kind of choices that women should avoid being involved in. But that is not always the case. I think it's also important to note that sometimes a man fails because the woman he is with doesn't really understand how to love or be in love with a man. Just as some women fail because the men they are with don't understand how to love or be in love with a woman. Sometimes the problems you have in your relationship are because of the person you are in the relationship with. Not that they caused the problems or are to blame for them. It's just that they are the wrong person, unless their partner knows how to turn that around. When a woman doesn't understand how to treat a man beyond having sex, she sets herself up for challenges in her relationship. These challenges could be avoided if she were informed. If she knows how men develop, how they think, how they process emotions and how they love, she will be so much better off. So that's what I'm trying to do—inform you!

ACCEPTING CHANGE

Men also fail because they don't know how to change and make transitions. Men don't like change much. They prefer doing the same thing over and over again in the same way. Yes, maybe they have a conversion experience and maybe they cut out the cursing and the drinking, but there's not much impact on their whole personality. So when God raises them to a new level or gives them a new experience, they revert back to doing things the way they did at the previous level— even if they give lip service to a desire to move forward. That

11: When Men Fail

just doesn't work! In the words so famously attributed to Einstein, "The definition of insanity is doing the same thing over and over and expecting different results."[15] You can't do the same things you used to do when God takes you up a step. You have to be able to handle drastic change.

I suggest that men get acquainted with change, because change is inevitable. No matter how much more comfortable he might be with the status quo, ultimately, he is going to change whether he wants to or not. Not only will he change, but you will also change. So start taking advantage of the level you're at now before things change.

> [16] *For a righteous man falls seven times, and rises again, But the wicked stumble in time of calamity.*
> **(Proverbs 24:16)**

---

[15] Atributed to various authors, including Albert Einstein and Benjamin Franklin.

12

MOVING HIM FROM LOGIC TO LOCOMOTION

My wife and I were enjoying a beautiful evening as we walked around the lake reminiscing on some the greatest moments of our relationship. As I listened to her and watched her smile, I got lost in the conversation. Initially I wanted to impress her with my intelligence—you know, make sure I said the right things to wow her. That worked for a minute or so, but then something happened. I began to slip from the clever words in my head into the feelings of my heart and I couldn't stop it from happening. One of the things I noticed was that the more I fell from my head into my heart, the less I said. The feelings were there, but the words just would not come.

At the time, we had been together for a while and I knew that she enjoyed an intellectually stimulating conversation. That was something I was good at—it was easy for me. But every now and then my heart would just jump in the way and I would find I was entirely in the moment, so much so that I was at a loss for words! When it came to expressing my deep feeling for her and our relationship, I was tongue-tied!

My wife—wonderfully sensitive and caring woman that she is—realized that something was happening inside of me, so she spoke to me as if I were student in a first grade classroom and what she said rang clear as a bell in my mind. My wife helped me learn to do what I had always failed to trust in myself—to go deep to where my innermost thoughts lay hidden and then bring those feelings to the surface and express them out loud. She said, "Use your words."

I thought to myself, "Use your words; *my* words; *all* my words; keep talking; talk more; talk deep; say what you cannot reach…" I went on and on in my head until finally I realized that, above everything, it was my *words* that she wanted. Imagine that: not the way I looked; not how strong I was or how I carried myself; not even how good a friend I was. It was my *words*. So I tried—slowly and hesitantly, but I did try. And as I struggled to express my deep feelings, I realized she not only wanted my words, she *needed* them. She patiently waited for them. She listened for them. Whether it was about something painful or whether it was a celebration, whatever "it" was, she wanted to hear me express it. She wanted to hear me promise it. She wanted to hear me confess it. Ultimately, for us, it was the words we spoke to each other that were our hope. Our words were our strength and it was *my* words that were my bond. And they still are!

Nothing binds a man more than the words that come out of his own mouth. Most men don't really understand this. They say things off the cuff and they say things that they don't intend to follow through on, not realizing how pregnant with potential for misinterpretation are the meanings packaged up in their words. Yes, a man's words are his bond. People expect that from him. His mother hoped it for him. The women he meets demand it of him. His children hold him to it. Life will always conclude that he means what he says until he proves it to be different.

12: Moving Him From Logic to Locomotion

ESSENTIALS MEN NEED TO LEARN

"It's a woman's prerogative to change her mind."

I'm sure you've heard that said many times. Maybe you've even used it as an excuse for doing an about-face on occasion. But, unlike women, men are not granted the liberty of changing their minds regarding how they feel about something or what they promise. Children will let their mother get away with saying "yes" only to say "no" a few minutes later to the same request, but they will always hold their father to his promises.

So in developing their communication skills, men have to learn two things that are essential for great relationships.

First, they have to move out of their heads and into their hearts. By this I mean that they have to be able to reach into their hearts and learn to attach deep passion and purpose to their promises. It's one thing to speak from your head when you tell your daughter that you love her. It's another thing to tell her that you love her while reaching deep into yourself to find the feeling of *why* you love her—while thinking of how precious a gift she is to you; how you wish for her all the things you are and more. When a man reaches in and speaks out, miracles happen. Men need to learn how to command from the inside. They have to grab hold of the thing in them that their *mothers* nurtured and bring that voice forward. It may be difficult at first, but it's everything the people that love him are waiting for.

When you ask a man how he feels, he may only be able to tell you what he thinks. Men are thinkers and their thoughts are their "intellectual property." But their feelings are hidden as the "emotional property" of their soul. Feelings are filtered through their head and they are rarely able to get to them without making a real effort. It's not that they don't want to feel but, rather, that feelings are hard to reach because men are not "wired" that way. Men are challenged by this paradox when they run into situations that force them to the ocean floor of their emotions. When tears are hard to hold back and anger is crying for revenge and violence, men rush to rescue these feelings with logic—calculated thought that gives rise to stability and control. If anything is ever important for a man, it is to always be in control of his emotions. Feeling is a dance they fear participating in because thinking is safer and more promising. Thinking keeps them from the explosive realities of their emotions. So, it's not that men don't feel, it's just that they don't feel in the same, easy way women feel.

This brings up an interesting question: if men don't handle their feelings like women do, are they doing something wrong?

The answer, of course, is no. Men don't have to do things like women to connect with women. And that is the second thing men need to learn: to accept that the way they are "wired" is o.k. Somewhere along the line, men have acquired the perception that there is something wrong with them. The way they sorted through sexual development by exploring as many girls as possible; the way they perceived their realities and responded to their environments; the way they sought attention and popularity; the way they ran from their responsibility when life left them with no resolve; the way they cried without tears because they really loved the things they lost—it may be true that most men haven't handled these situations appropriately. But there is nothing wrong with their *manhood*, there is something wrong with *life* and men have had to try to figure it all out and find where they fit in at the same time they are actually living it. And more likely than not, they didn't have the tools; or, to make things even more confusing, they had the *wrong* tools to begin with.

12: Moving Him From Logic to Locomotion

WHOSE RESPONSIBILITY IS IT?

Where does the responsibility lie for restoring men to leadership and ownership of their manhood? With the individual man or with those around him—the environment he lives in? Society stripped away so much, so fast! Somehow sociological progression of the past few decades led to men regressing at the cost of their families. They felt they lost everything they once had authority over.

Men are not bad. They are not lost.

They are lonely. They are tired. They are confused.

When men now in their 30s and 40s were growing up, even the churches and Sunday school classes were feminine in nature and the schools they attended were geared towards non-aggressive interactions and soft talk. And their women? Well, all too frequently their women have written these men off as irresponsible seed-sowers with no other significance. Courts have determined that they make bad parents, compared to women. The world of commerce has concluded that sex is an easy sell and has used men for nothing more than capital gain. Is it no wonder that so many men feel powerless and inconsequential, making them easy prey to the immediate gratification of sleazy sex, drugs and crime? So, men are not lost. Men are lonely. Whether they give up the battle for their manhood or struggle to hang on to it, either way they feel that they are on their own.

Yet one of the greatest, most powerful institutions capable of restoring men to their true manhood is that of marriage and family. Women stand at the pinnacle of their rescue. Women can love men back to life because real men want nothing more than a reason to belong to someone or something. So ladies, love your husband like he's the most fabulous, fascinating, sexy man in the world. Cultivate an environment that reaches him deeply and draws his heart towards yours. Give him a touch that reminds him that life is not over yet. Look at him as though your life depends on his success. Get behind him, beside him, underneath him, and even above him when he needs to be pulled forward. But most of all get *inside* him. You will find things there that will assuage even your own insecurities. Cry the tears that won't fall from his eyes. Literally, put your teary cheek on his so he feels your deep empathy. He's been struggling too long and he knows that this marriage may be the only chance he has to find his own life.

THE GUILTY MAN

Some men feel so guilty! They feel like they have failed their families, the people who loved them, the people who depended on them and everyone and everything else. Because of their competitive nature, men are often acutely, painfully aware of the fact that they have not done as well as they had planned. Regardless of how it might look in reality, even a man who appears to be successful outwardly will always try to do something about the fact that he didn't reach the goals he set for himself. One of the things such men do best is to make false and guilt-driven promises. And here's the thing: more often than not, they believe their own promises—at least at the time.

Let your son know as he is growing up that he doesn't need to make promises to compensate for his insecurities. Teach him that buying what he can't afford or boasting about how he's going to get some fantastic "toy" in the future is not the sign of a true man. Because when he is a grown, it's one thing to want the best for his children and family, but it's another thing to get in trouble buying things he can't afford. Buying an expensive car, for instance, showing it off and allowing the kids and family to get the most enjoyment out of it as possible, all along knowing that at some point the bank is going to come pick it up, just adds to his self-reproach. Living with a guilty conscience puts too much pressure on the soul of a man. It creates a vicious circle, producing more actions to feel guilty about and promoting behaviors that are unwanted, undesirable and unhealthy.

FROM MIND TO MUSCLE

How can men connect with the people they love and who really love them? They need to learn to move what is in their Mind to their Muscle.

Let me explain.

Men use logic in most of their day-to-day situations. Men make decisions cautiously. They don't give too much too fast. They make sure that they balance the give-and-take dynamics in a relationship. They are always conscious of what's going out and what's coming in. They are logical, calculating creatures. The problem is that this logic doesn't always translate to action. What I mean is that men don't follow up on what they think. They don't make their logic locomotive. They are missing an essential part of the process.

When a man and women start to think seriously of forming a lasting relationship, they go at it differently. Women think of men with their bodies—i.e., with their emotions. They come from the heart. But when a man thinks about the woman he wants as a permanent partner, he thinks about her with his brain—i.e., he uses logic to weigh the pros and cons of such a bond. And once they are married, he tends to continue thinking about the relationship in logical terms. He treats it like he would a business.

Yet, deep inside he does have a heart and if he wants to create a bond with his wife strong enough to last over the years, he needs to recognize his deep-rooted feelings and learn how to move those feelings into conscious expression. Men need to be able to genuinely and honestly express themselves. They need to be able to think good thoughts and move those thoughts into concrete measurable behaviors that reflect exactly what they intend.

Let's use the story of Adam in the Garden of Eden to help explain this concept—specifically, Adam's conversation with God about eating the forbidden fruit (Genesis 3:8-12).

> [8] They heard the sound of the LORD God walking in the garden in the cool of the day, and the man and his wife hid themselves from the presence of the LORD God among the trees of the garden. [9] Then the LORD God called to the man, and said to him, "Where are you?" [10] He said, "I heard the sound of You in the garden, and I was afraid because I was naked; so I hid myself." [11] And He said, "Who told you that you were naked? Have you eaten from the tree of which I commanded you not to eat?" [12] The man said, "The woman whom You gave *to be* with me, she gave me from the tree, and I ate."

12: Moving Him From Logic to Locomotion

A Closer Look:

What Happened	What Was It	Where I Was
I heard…	Thy voice…	In the garden…

What I Felt	Why I Felt That Way	My Response
I was afraid…	because I was naked…	I hid myself…

This passage of scripture literally lays out for us one of the greatest challenges men forever face as a result of Adam's fall—a problem Adam obviously didn't have prior to his disobedience of God.

First of all, we must understand that the initial onset of the problem occurred when Adam heard something. Hearing is critical and listening is a skill that men must develop for several reasons. Adam's problem didn't begin with his heart or his eyes. It began with what he heard. Most of what men struggle with is because of what they hear. Knowledge, logic and even faith all begin with hearing.

There is a space between hearing and acting, or what I call "logic and locomotion." For Adam, the action he took was to hide; but before he hid, he *heard*. Between his hearing (logic) and his hiding (locomotion), several other things happened. Initially, he perceived that his nakedness was inappropriate for coming face-to-face with his Creator. As a result, he felt fear—for the first time in his life! So he took action and hid to avoid the consequences of having given in to temptation. But, of course, God, being omniscient, omnipresent and omnipotent, didn't let Adam (or Eve, or the serpent) get away with that!

For a man there is a space between logic and locomotion as well. What occurs in this space is what I call the "filtering process." In this process we find emotional responses to internal interpretations. Adam's emotional response was that he was afraid. His perception of himself was that he was naked. His fear was not the reverent awe of God's presence or having communion with God, which he had enjoyed so many times before, but rather of the things he was now thinking and feeling about himself as a result of eating from the tree of knowledge of good and evil. The two fundamental things that would impact his actions were his own *perception* and his *feelings about* those perceptions.

Men need to be more consciously aware of what they are thinking and how those thoughts make them feel, because this will always determine how they react.

Since Adam could not hide from God because of God's omniscience and omnipresence, Adam hid from himself. Exactly what was he hiding? He wasn't hiding his body, but he was hiding the "self"—that internal living, breathing soul that needs the redemption of God. This is the part of a man that carries the deep interpretations of his experiences and his physical life. That part of him that is so hard for the people who love him to reach. That part of him that he himself can't even get close to. That naked part of him. That vulnerable part of him. Most men know what I'm talking about.

Adam was literally hiding himself from himself, because it is impossible to hide from God. When men wear masks, they don't do it to hide their true self from others, but rather to hide their conscious psyche from themselves. Men feel safer when they can hide the "self" from themselves. It helps them to hide their nakedness, so that what they present to the world and what other people see is only their "dressed up" side. Of course, it's not only men who have this problem—almost everyone does.

Adam was ashamed and shame damages the relationship you have with God and the relationship you have with yourself. Men who feel shame may suffer from the following conditions:

1. Fear of being vulnerable and exposing themselves.
2. Fear of intimacy and avoidance of real commitment in relationships.
3. Feeling defensive even from minor negative feedback.
4. Seeing mistakes as imperfections.
5. Blaming others.
6. Feeling controlled by the outside and from within; they block normal spontaneous expressions.
7. Lying to themselves and others.
8. Getting stuck in dependence and co-dependence.
9. Having limited emotional boundaries.
10. Using rage, withdrawal, isolation or people-pleasing to build false boundaries.
11. Perfectionism—feeling that they have to do things perfectly or not at all.
12. Extreme shyness and feelings of inferiority.
13. Being critical of the qualities of others that they feel ashamed of in themselves.
14. Feeling ugly inside and therefore acting ugly towards others.

When a mother is absent in a child's life, the child may experience an extreme level of sadness, but when the father is absent, the child often feels deep shame, which can remain severely detrimental for a long time because it so difficult to overcome. That's another reason why a father's presence in a boy's life is so important.

It is so hard for men to take responsibility for their inner self and learn to love their whole self. Men need to realize that Adam's dilemma didn't end with the insightful process of realizing that he was ashamed of his nakedness and so hid his "self." They need to also recognize that God always confronts this type of behavior. God asks questions that directly address this kind of action. God asked Adam what was said, who said it and what happened? Not because He didn't know already, but because the only way to reach an uncommitted, unaccountable man—even the very first man—is to ask commitment questions and demand answers. Adam didn't answer the first question and evaded the second. Nevertheless, through questioning, God determined what limits and boundaries he needed to set for Adam to put him on the course to personal redemption and restoration.

> [19] *By the sweat of your face*
> *You will eat bread,*
> *Till you return to the ground,*
> *Because from it you were taken;*
> *For you are dust,*
> *And to dust you shall return.*
> **(Genesis 3:19)**

In helping men move from logic to locomotion, I actually guide them away from their minds into their muscles (from a thought to an action). I help them go from thinking to doing and position them to conquer the highest mountains of their dreams. Men need this desperately.

12: Moving Him From Logic to Locomotion

Lastly, men need to become conscious of how they filter situations and what they filter things through. The more conscious a man is of knowing how he filters information, the more equipped he will be in moving from logic to locomotion.

If you are married or in love with a man, you know exactly what I mean. A woman can do so much more than have sex with a man. She can help him get to the space between logic and locomotion by grasping how the filtering laboratory works, she can help him to process, feel and make sense of his inner self and encourage him to put what he learns into action. The closer she is to this place in him, the better she will understand and be able to connect with him.

> [14] *What use is it, my brethren, if someone says he has faith but he has no works? Can that faith save him?*
> **(James 2:14)**

13

LONG ROADS AND DEAD ENDS

Life teaches us what to do and what not to do, but only if we are paying attention. If your guy finds himself on a road that leads to nowhere, it's probably because he missed the signs along the way warning him of a dead end ahead. Most men don't want directions and the rest of them don't read directions when they have them. Men have their own ideas about how things work, how things should be put together and where things are headed. They'd rather pretend to be knowledgeable about something of which they are totally ignorant than be given instructions by a woman, even when she's right and they know it.

An unplanned life—an inattentive life—leads to dead ends. God uses situations in a man's lifetime to teach him important lessons. When men don't pay attention to these moments, they make a lot of mistakes. Sometimes these are the same mistakes they've made previously, because men simply don't use their experience to learn about healthy choices. I always tell the men I counsel they should never make the same mistake twice. Because life is based on choices and success is tied to the choices we make; repeating the same mistake is like butting your head against a wall over and over again.

One of the reasons men find themselves at dead ends is because either they are focused on only one goal or they widen their focus but then put their energy into things that won't help them get to their goals.

Men in the first category are sometimes so inflexible that, if they don't reach their goal, they feel defeated. They only want one thing and their identity is wound so tightly around it, if it doesn't work, they have a really hard time rebounding. These men need to learn to shoot at broader, more diversified targets. They need to always have a Plan B ready, and maybe a Plan C and a Plan D as well.

CHOOSING TO WORK

I tell men constantly that the time for chasing dreams is during childhood. I don't suggest they keep on chasing their dreams as adults. I tell them, "You must look at your life and see where you have given your best efforts. What are the areas of your life where you used your personal gifts and received the best return for your actions? When you know where that is, pour more of yourself into that area. That way you're not just chasing a dream or an ideal, you're actually pursuing a goal through measurable efforts. Thinking this way will shorten those long roads and eliminate your dead ends."

Now, I'm not saying not to work. Nor do I say overwork. I simply suggest that men put their energy in the place where they'll get the biggest return on their investment of time and effort. There is nothing wrong with testing the waters, but at the end of the day they want to make sure they are investing in the right things. What does this mean? It means they have to work and they have to work hard.

Sometimes a man has to "work harder than all the rest to be the best." Work is what real men do. It's what they are made for. The Bible says a man who doesn't work, doesn't eat. Not only does he not eat natural food, but he also doesn't consume the nourishment and benefits of a healthy, productive life. A man who has no motivation to work will find himself getting depressed and withdrawing from the people around him. Eventually he will turn to pornography, drugs, overeating, crime, suicide or some other means of escape.

Men are producers and have been since God created Adam ("¹⁵ Then the LORD God took the man and put him into the garden of Eden to cultivate it and keep it." Genesis 2:15). As discussed in Chapter 4—Inside a Man's World, men love projects. Men are made for production and being engaged in some kind of production is one of the most critical elements of manhood. That's why they treat everything they have like a project, including—if they don't know better—girlfriends, wives and children.

But these men don't just want the product; they want a functional product—one that does something. They want to be able to look at it, touch it, wind it up and make it do what it does. Men are fascinated with the way things work. They are investigative and all about control. Like little boys, at times they are amazed at how much fun they can have controlling a productive product.

Take the remote for example. It changes the channel, but do you have to watch every channel just because you have the remote? It's not really about watching TV for men. It's about letting that television know: "I can watch all of you and as much of you, however and whenever I want to. And I can turn you on and off. I can change you. I can mute you; turn you up; turn you down or do whatever else I want with you."

What power! What control!

O.k., the remote is just a symbol, but holding it feels like power and men love power. A man loves being in charge of his environment, especially when being in charge feels productive—especially if, at the end of the day, he feels like he has accomplished something. That's the thing men want the most. They want to accomplish something.

FLEXIBILITY BREEDS SUCCESS

Focus is important when working towards a goal, but so is flexibility. When men are so focused on a particular goal that they go through life like a horse with blinkers on, seeing only what is straight in front of them, they will miss opportunities that could have an even better outcome. Then, when the road they are on turns into a dead end, they begin to lose hope and stamina. Men with a broader vision understand that sometimes the long, narrow road leads to a dead end. So they avoid getting stuck on one thing. They are ready to turn. Ready to change direction at any time. Ready to hear from God at any moment. They give things a period of testing and then they make decisions about the future.

Successful men try different things and then put their major efforts into the area where they get the best return. For example, imagine an engineer working as a consultant with clients across the country, when what he really wants is to become a Life or Business Coach. His best plan of action will be to evaluate his efforts (output) in both the engineering field and in coaching and measure that against his return (input). Where is the money coming from? What is paying the bills? Which area has the greatest return in terms of income or personal satisfaction? Once he has this information in front of him, he can decide to put more effort into the areas of his life that bring in the most measurable benefits. This way, whichever

13: Long Roads and Dead Ends

career he settles on, he will feel that sense of accomplishment from seeing the positive results of his labors.

The more focused and strategic a man is, the better he will be at making sure he can handle these long roads and dead ends. But remember, it's focused with flexibility. He will learn to have patience when things take longer than he anticipated. He will not become discouraged when he has turn around and go back the other way.

What does a smart man do to avoid going too long in a direction that eventually leads to a dead end? He involves himself in gathering information about whatever he's working on by networking and connecting with other people who are experts in that area. Placing himself in the midst of a multitude of wise, experienced and well-informed people will help him make his own smart decisions. No man is an island—"it is not good for Adam to be alone."

Psalm 119:105 says: "Thy word is a lamp unto my feet, and a light unto my path." Examine that verse carefully. Which shines brighter: the lamp of God's word on your feet or the full blown light of God's word on your path? Some men are so focused on the path ahead that they miss where they are putting their feet and others are so focused on their feet that they miss seeing where the path is leading. You have to be able to do both—see the long-term vision and monitor your progress towards it. Wise men make evaluations at both levels. The first level, the feet, is just as critical as the second, the path. Feet represent the here and now. They symbolize what is currently happening and what the man is currently doing in both his public and private life.

The lamp represents a man's ability to take responsibility for where he is (his feet), even though he doesn't have total long-term vision for a future. The first step is knowing where you are and accepting responsibility for the present, even before you journey into the future.

This is true of both men and women, of course. Monitoring your feet can prevent you from falling into sin that so easily besets you. It helps to see where your toes are pointed, how they are pointed, how quickly or slowly they are moving and how clean or dirty they have become. Many men with great vision fall to sin, not because they haven't seen the long term light of their vision, but because they failed to pay attention to the daily details of their life that exist under the focused lamp of God's word.

The second level, the light, is the full illumination that allows a man to see where he should go. So the lamp lets him see where he is and the light helps him to see where he is going. The full illuminated light of God's word is not for the feet, but rather for the path. That's why it's so important that men have vision because, without the full illumination of long-term vision, a man is left with only a small circle of lamplight at his feet. Without this path men will perish. The problem with so many Christian men is that they don't have a decisive long-term vision. They cannot see a long-term path, so they settle for satisfying a yearning for delights with immediate gratification—engaging in things that are temporal rather than eternal.

When men couple the lamp of watching their current life with making sure it is pointing in the direction of their long-term path illuminated by the word of God, they save themselves and the ones who love them from the destructive tactics of the enemy.

LOCATION, LOCATION, LOCATION

God never calls a man to Himself. He always calls a man to a destination. Men need to foresee their destiny and design their lives to match that destiny. Men need to think of vision in terms of property or location. They need to think in terms of real estate. Not just what God wants me to do, but *where* he wants me to do it.

Real estate is called *real* estate for a reason—because it's tangibly real. So when a man thinks of God calling him to something, it is very important to determine where it is He's calling them to. Most men make the mistake of saying God called them to do something but they have no idea about where they are supposed to do it. Your location is just as important as what you're doing and can often make, or hinder, or break your vision.

The same is true with dating or looking for the right woman. That magic doesn't just happen. Well, at least on the larger scale. Sure, some men are lucky enough to be in the right place at the right time, but for most of us it's about getting to where the good girls are. It's location, location, location.

God always calls a man to a particular place when calling him to a certain mission. So men have to answer the location question to ensure they have themselves and their families in the place where God wants to bless them. What city will you live in? What church will you go to? What neighborhood will you give your time to? Vision becomes tangible when a man decides where his base of operations will be. Deciding where you will locate yourself is sometimes the difference between success and failure; and sometimes the question of location is the greatest leap of faith a man will ever take.

When men fail to consider their location, they often find themselves going from job to job or from one vocation to the next—or sometimes from one woman to the next—with no real stability because they have not crystalized the vision of what they want to do and where they want to be while doing it.

Finally, it is important to remember that where you are when you answer your calling needs to be God's decision and not yours. (In the next chapter, you can read my personal story of how God called me to the state of Louisiana following Hurricane Katrina.) Men sometimes have a difficult time making decisions that are based strictly on God's will for their life, because they are too tied up in impressing other people or making them happy. Men are busy looking for father figures and for approval from other people and that limits their ability to really do well for God. Nor do they like taking responsibility for their failures—it's easier to blame the women in their life. What they really need is a woman who makes them accountable in the sense that she asks about where they are going, what they will do, and where they will live? When women ask men questions of vision, they help promote the accountability that men need. Women should do this gracefully—not pressuring him, but at least asking and dreaming together with him.

> [11] *I again saw under the sun that the race is not to the swift and the battle is not to the warriors, and neither is bread to the wise nor wealth to the discerning nor favor to men of ability; for time and chance overtake them all.*
> **(Ecclesiastes 9:11)**

14

FUNNEL LIVING

PAYING IT FORWARD

During a very challenging move to Louisiana after Hurricane Katrina, I was experiencing God in a whole new way. I had learned to trust God beyond what seemed logical. I was developing the kind of faith that trusted His will and not just His voice. The best word to explain the state I was in is "vulnerable." And I mean *very* vulnerable. My heart was torn by the catastrophe of Hurricane Katrina, as it was for so many other people who witnessed that cataclysmic event.

I began praying prayers I had never prayed before. I began seeing visions and having dreams of young children carrying grown people three times their weight over their heads to keep them from drowning. When I first visited the area, I realized that the dreams were not very far from reality. I don't know if you have ever been broken by something that had nothing to do with you. I don't know if you have empathized so deeply with people that you actually became one with them and their grief and pain became yours.

That's how I felt. I couldn't really understand what was happening in my heart, but I knew that my dozen years as a professional counselor did not prepare me for this. I was either losing my mind or burning out in my profession. I tried pulling things together for myself, but the more I resisted and set therapeutic boundaries, the more the Lord began to press upon my heart for the State of Louisiana. So one day I decided that I would relocate to that state by joining Desire Street Ministries, a New Orleans-based ministry founded by Pastor Mo Leverett at a time when the lower 9th ward of New Orleans was rated as the murder capital of the United States.

I remembered sitting in one of Pastor Leverett's classes as he taught us about poverty. I began to cry when he talked about Jesus's descent into our earthly community, describing how the word became flesh and "dwelt" among us. I remember the pastor saying that Jesus "left the best to be joined to the rest." And that rest included me. I wept uncontrollably and had to leave the class because all of my life I had dreamed of becoming great—of chasing an American dream, moving out of my family's single-parent home and make really BIG things happen for myself. I was always told to get out of the small rural town I had grown up in and become something. I was always taught to leave, to escape and not let the barriers of my environment limit me to that area. Now I was hearing Mo Leverett say, "Come back." I was hearing him say "Your place is more beautiful than America will ever know." He was telling me that the impoverished, crime-infested neighborhoods of my youth held a secret and that secret was extraordinarily great people. That beautiful people lived there. That brilliant children lived there. God, did he give me new perspective!

I later met a Christian philanthropist who had donated hundreds of thousands of dollars to Desire Street Ministries. I was having dinner with him and relating the story of my upbringing. As he in turn began to share about his own childhood, I realized that his pains were greater than mine. Since this gentleman was white and fairly wealthy, I had initially assumed that his life was privileged. I was so wrong. His current life was simply the result of a decision to work hard and dream big. He said something to me that night that would crystalize the things that God was doing in my heart and that God wanted me to understand.

After we had finished our meal he asked if he could pray for us. I replied, "Sure." He closed a very short prayer by asking God to give him more so that he could continue to give it away. "Give it away," I thought. "Who does that?" Who asks for more so that they can give more away? *He* did and I felt my heart melt. I drove away from his home that night bothered by everything I had ever thought about money, education, business and success.

Later that week in devotion I began to talk to the Lord and I remember saying words that caused me to pause, cry and reflect on the entire move to Louisiana. I asked the Lord to expand the territory of my heart before he expanded the territory of my hand; to open my heart to giving before he gave me more. I wanted big hands, but I wanted a big heart first. I began to mature from one level of manhood to the next. God was moving me up that step. I realized that life is not about how much you make, but how much of what you make that you actually give away—literally, to live like a funnel, so that all the good that is poured into you from every direction is channeled into a clear, focused stream that flows out and away from you to the world. That whatever you get, you give. If you get more, give more.

Imagine that for a second. Imagine your life as a funnel. Whatever is going in, is coming out. Whatever God blesses you with, you are intentionally and strategically using to bless others. Men need to understand that God wants to give them abundance so they can contribute to society by giving it back. A man who doesn't have a broader reason to become successful than for his own benefit is missing out on God's intent for his life.

THE DEVIL MADE ME DO IT!

Men are often tempted by pride, personal gain and selfishness and don't even realize they are being manipulated. As a matter of fact, the devil doesn't usually tempt men directly. The devil is always using other people or situations to tempt men to move away from the things God wants them to do. Christ was tempted by Peter, Adam by Eve and Job by his wife.

Men have to ask themselves, "How is the devil tempting me or who is he using to tempt me?" Temptation can pull you toward the idea that you don't have to give back, that you have to hold on to what you have because you worked so hard for it. That other people's misfortune is because of their own failure.

This temptation is a dangerous one because it contradicts everything scripture teaches us about salvation itself. It was Christ who gave. It was Christ who saved. It was Christ who died. And He did it all for you. He poured Himself out and into your life so that you can *have* a life. As a matter of fact, you wouldn't even be able to bear the trials of your life unless He gave you the grace to do so. So our aim in life should be getting to give, not giving to get. Cast the devil aside and let the good stuff flow through your funnel.

LOVING FROM THE INSIDE OUT

Let me say it again: Men have a hard time expressing their deep inner feelings. They have to learn the "heart stuff" that happens on the inside—it doesn't come naturally, the deep conversations; the profound emotional expressions and connections that lead to excellent relationships.

14: Funnel Living

Sometimes men feel like they will lose part of their manhood if they do the heart stuff. They often feel like it's soft and less manly than the things that men normally identify as masculine. Most men *want* the soft stuff; they just haven't learned how to *do* the soft stuff. That is not to say that they can't do it; but they just aren't motivated enough to do the hard work that soft stuff requires. They have no idea what they are missing!

Encourage your menfolk to grasp that in actuality they won't lose their hard, manly stuff just because they share their soft inner stuff. This may be something that a father can't give to his sons, but you can. Think of the difference between a coach and a counselor. The coach yells, screams and guides from the outside and the counselor softly reflects on feelings on the inside. Between them, they help the internal and external combine into a powerful whole.

Especially when a man has no conquering drive to expose his vulnerable, soft side, you can help him see there are rewards down the road. For example if you're dating a man whose ultimate desire is to sleep with you, he might seem to be a perfect at the soft stuff because he has an agenda. But once he accomplishes his mission, it becomes more difficult for him to continue sharing that same soft stuff with you because he doesn't see the point—he already got what he wanted. That's why a woman should keep holding out "goodies" in front of him. If he is your husband, make him chase after something. Make him want you. You might be surprised at how happy you can be if you manage your goodies well. If the two of you are not yet in a committed relationship, this is one way you can gage whether the guy can sustain the soft stuff over the long haul.

As you observe your man struggling with this, you can provide him with a safe space for exposing his vulnerabilities. Let him know that you love him as he is, that you are not trying to change him; you are there to show through your example that when he dares to give you the gift of his inner thoughts and feelings, he will be compensated in ways he may never have imagined.

As a mother, you can do the same for your son. Let him know that his inner feelings are a valid part of his whole self and that it takes a brave boy to show his emotions; it sure doesn't make him a "sissy!"

When men learn to conduct their lives in "funnel fashion," they learn to connect with their inside and allow the insight they gather from the inside to reach the outside. They learn that the things that are poured into their life must come out through their life. They become less afraid of the soft stuff because they know that it's what really matters. A man who has learned this is better able to connect with his wife, sons, daughters and the other significant people in his life.

> [38] *Give, and it will be given to you. They will pour into your lap a good measure—pressed down, shaken together,* and *running over. For by your standard of measure it will be measured you in return.*
> **(Luke 6:38)**

15

SAVING OUR SONS

In a society devoid of fathers, young boys are destined to become men one way or another. What can they do to ensure they get the things they need to survive in life? Do they need mentors or do they need mediators? Do they need baby-sitters who tell them good stories about their own life or do they need men who point out to them realities of their lives? Do they need positive men or do they need their own fathers? Is there a difference? And if there is a difference, how do we make true Godly adult males of boys lacking the presence in their lives of the men who co-created them?

FROM MENTORS TO MEDIATORS

For a long time the practice of mentoring has given fatherless boys and boys who need positive role models in their lives an opportunity to experience what they otherwise would miss out on. Unfortunately, more often than not, the mentors themselves grew up fatherless and are resolving their own issues of fatherlessness by sowing seeds into the next generation of fatherless boys.

You see, when a fatherless boy becomes a man and begins to mentor another fatherless boy, he draws that kid to himself. He shows that youngster how he made it through the obstacles created by not having a father as a positive presence in his life. Like a magnet, the young kid is drawn to him. The mentor quiets his personal insecurities through the child he is mentoring, rather than confronting his own father—whether in real life or in his mind. Most mentors will agree that it feels good when young people look up to you and are inspired by your life and influence. But I want to challenge the concept of mentoring by sharing a new perspective that I believe could change the course of mentoring as dramatically as Steve Jobs changed the telephone, computer and music market, and that is that mentors must become mediators.

There are three distinct components in the paradigm shift from mentors to mediators. What exactly is a mediator and how is a mediator different from a mentor? According to the dictionary, to "mediate" is "to act as an intermediary, especially to seek to resolve (differences) between two or more conflicting parties." Consulting a Thesaurus, we see that a "mediator" is a "conciliator," "go-between," "intercessor," and "peacemaker," while a "mentor" is one who "give[s] advice and instruction to (someone) regarding the course or process to be followed"—a coach, counselor, leader, pilot, shepherd, or tutor. I would like to add my own definitions here, because I see mentors as "Rescue Workers" and mediators as "Workers of Redemption."

All of these definitions fall within the framework of what I call Kingdom Priorities, which I define as those things we hold important because of our biblical convictions: (1) the Family, (2) Redemption and (3) Reconciliation.

1. THE FAMILY

A healthy family is one of the core elements of Kingdom Priorities. The ultimate objective of a family is not just to exist and produce children, but also to influence and impact the world for God. Families carry out the will of God through their own giftedness. The purpose of family order is to bring peace so that the family can fulfill its mission in the most focused and impactful way possible. Therefore, God sets the order for children, mothers and fathers as outlined in the section on Redemptive Son-ship discussed earlier in the book. I want you to think about this. God not only wants you to have a family, but he wants your family to be at peace. Literally, He wants to bring "shalom" to the family system.

Often when we help children by providing service and support alone, we miss the ultimate intent of God. God wants to bring shalom—peace, and this is where a mediator can help. I remember working for the Department of Children & Family Services during my earlier years as a counselor. There were three distinct divisions in the department, each serving a different role, but all endeavoring to ultimately resolve the problems presented by a family. It was the responsibility of the Protective Services Department to remove from the home children who were allegedly abused, neglected or abandoned and place them in state custody. Once they were in custody, the Foster Care Division, which is where I worked, developed a plan to reunite the child with its biological family. In the event the child and his or her family were not able to be brought back together, the Adoption Division pursued the termination of parental rights and successful adoptive placement of the child.

Spencer's Story

In my role, I ensured that everything possible was done to give parents an opportunity to correct problems and prove that they were capable of successfully raising their children. I remember a particular case that really helped to shape my perspective of the innate connection children have with their biological parents. We'll call the child in question "Spencer." Spencer was a 13-year-old black kid who was removed from his mother's home due to neglect. For most of his life Spencer had lived independent of his mother's supervision because of her drug addiction. This youngster was quite amazing, resilient and lovable. He had learned how to ration food, steal power from city electric lines and navigate in the dark by using touch and smell. Spencer mentioned that his father was in prison. At least that's what his mother told him. He had never actually met his dad.

Spencer's maturity was quite interesting. He had already begun having sex, served as a watch for local drug dealers and had even learned to sell drugs himself. Spencer was able to hold adult conversations and ask mature questions. He wasn't fearful of his future and appeared to be strong and determined on the outside.

One day in therapy Spencer was fiddling with a toy truck and rolled it away from the play area. When asked where he went, he said, "I left...I'm far away." Spencer wanted to be away from the life he was living. He wanted to be far away from that life. Then he began crying and shaking and said, "I have to go back and get my mother." At such a young age and after all his mother had put him through due to her drug addiction, he still wanted to go and get her.

When asked where he wanted to live, Spencer would always say with his mother. There was something inside of him that, regardless of how hard his mother had made his life, still held on to the love he had for her. He never made excuses for her; he just wanted to make sure that he was with her.

What does that say to us? What does it tell us about biological child-parent bonds? Well, I think it says that the people God choses to be your parents will always have influence in your life. So it is important to recognize this bond and resolve issues between parents and children, even if they will never live together again.

I believe and want to propose to you that boys want their fathers just as badly as Spencer wanted his mother—that inside the heart of every young man is a deep need to be connected to his father. Placing Spencer in a foster or adoptive home was not enough. He needed the shalom/peace in his heart restored by making sure that he reconciled with his mother. This is just as true for boys with absent fathers. The only way to restore peace in their hearts is to confront and resolve the issues caused by their fathers not being present in their lives. However, most mentorship programs don't focus on this issue. Instead, they measure their success on the children's academic performance, whether they stay out of trouble, and how independent they become. If the boy can do that without any problem, then the adults feel the mentoring has worked. In reality, it has *not* worked if the boy has never resolved his interior issues; being successful on the outside is far from the whole story. It's the gaining of peace on the inside that is most important.

2. REDEMPTION

Most mentorship programs are designed to rescue boys from their environment and show them another way to live. Mentors feel successful if they have saved a young boy from becoming a statistic and from the mistakes that they themselves made in the past. That is all well and good, *and* we must go further—from Rescue Workers to becoming Workers of Redemption. Imagine you are that young, fatherless kid. A rescuer wants to save you from where you are now. A redemptive worker wants to join your life in a way and help you make the best out of your own resources. A rescuer wants to take you to their neighborhood and let you see their home.

A redemptive worker wants to see *your* home and understand more about how you are surviving. A rescuer wants to play the role of the dad you never had. A redemptive worker wants to introduce you to *your own dad* and help you resolve issues with your father. A rescuer wants you to see them as good. A redemptive worker wants you to see *your own parents* as good and helps to build a perspective about your parents that promotes healing and engagement. A rescuer wants to empower themselves through working with you. A redemptive worker wants to empower *you* by dethroning themselves. A rescuer sees your situation as a hindrance to your success. A redemptive worker sees that your environment has made you strong and that it can contribute to your success. A rescuer wants to shape your thinking based upon his or her own insecurities. A redemptive worker wants you to think for yourself. A rescuer wants to take you away from every sticky situation you're in. A redemptive worker wants to connect you to everything in a healthy way. Most rescuers, although they may not admit it, want to take you from your dad especially. A redemptive worker wants to bring you to your dad so you can deal with those issues. A rescuer sides with your mother about how bad your father is. A redemptive worker helps her understand how she has hindered you by cutting off your relationship with him.

That's the difference between mentors and what I call mediators. Mentors operate like rescuers, while mediators operate as workers of redemption. Mediators are constantly working to bring children back to their parents rather than pulling the children to themselves. They don't become surrogate fathers; they usher boys to their biological fathers while maintaining their own healthy relationships with these boys. Mentors can sometimes be in a child's life forever. Mediators are there only for a season. Their intent is not to become what we all know they can never be—a stand-in for an absent father, but to come in, accomplish their purpose and then leave. This helps a boy grow up whole and well defined in his self-identity and self-esteem. It also teaches him forgiveness, which is *the* primary tool used in redemptive mediation.

3. RECONCILIATION

A skilled mentor does not attempt to become a youngster's surrogate father; nor does he act as merely a role model. Mentors need to be trained as mediators and become involved in the work of reconciliation and empowerment for young men with absent fathers. They must deepen their emotional involvement and help the child heal from a poor or non-existent relationship with dad. When mentors serve as mediators they become agents of reconciliation.

Joyce's Story

A single mother, "Joyce," called my office as she desperately sought help for her 14-year-old son. The boy's father had been absent from his life for the last 12 years. During the interview Joyce said, "He really just needs a positive man in his life. I can only do so much. But he's growing up now and I just can't do it anymore." I asked her where the boy's father was and her response was, "I don't know. He's never been in his life and he's not good for him anyway." I paused and said, "He doesn't need a positive male role model. He needs his father."

Joyce looked at me with her eyebrows raised and said, "Well, that's not going to happen." She was shocked to hear me then tell her that it absolutely was going to happen and she was going to help me make it happen. Getting through her pain so that she could eventually help her son was harder for

Joyce than actually helping her son. But eventually she was able to do both.

Sometimes parents bring their children to therapy when they themselves need the help and this was one of those times. After six months, Joyce was able to reconcile the issues of her own broken heart and her son was able to separate his own anger towards his father from his mother's, making it easier for him to forgive his dad and reconcile their relationship.

MORE ON KINGDOM PRIORITIES

Let me explain further: Men who fail to prioritize their lives can never be successful. When they prioritize their lives, the energy they put in has to reciprocate what they are putting out so that they are not drained and overwhelmed and then go looking for the next woman or sexual experience to bail them out. They have to adopt Kingdom Priorities because real men (men who have accepted Christ as Savior and committed their lives to Him) belong to the Kingdom of God and not the kingdom of this world. And since they belong to the Kingdom of God, they need to function within the parameters of that kingship. That kingdom operates quite differently than the kingdom of the world. So a man's task in living out Kingdom Priorities is to first embrace the fact that he does not belong to himself, but rather to the King of this new kingdom. He is not at the mercy his own will but rather the will of his King. In determining what is most important for him, he has to determine what is important to his King.

You see, when a woman believes in God, it's almost expected; but when a man believes in God, the atmosphere shifts and things begin to change for everybody in the family. Because the headship of a man of faith shifts the entire atmosphere of the home. The family is set by leadership that moves it towards an ultimate Kingdom experience. Everybody wins under this scenario.

One of the hardest situations for a woman is when she believes and her husband doesn't. When she goes to church and her husband doesn't. When she tries to live out Kingdom Principles, but her man is still living in the world. Sometimes the clashes you're having are not personality clashes but rather Kingdom clashes—he believes one thing and you believe another. He's into the world and you may be into him, but the principles you hold true to don't fit where your love energy is being directed.

So a man has to prioritize his life or he will lose his life. He has to lead his life or he will be led by his life. He needs to ask himself: "What is most important and what am I going to do about it?" What comes first, what comes second and what comes after that? His focus needs to be on the priorities; everything else is secondary.

The three things that every man must prioritize are his faith—his relationship with God; his family—wife and kids; and his fellowship—who and what he gives his time to.

> *17 But the lovingkindness of the Lord is from everlasting to everlasting on those who fear Him, And His righteousness to children's children,*
> **(Psalms 103:17)**

16

CELEBRATING MANHOOD

As I prepare to put my pen down and close this book, I rest my heart from ten years' emotional pain concerning the state of manhood, from remembering

- how many of the men in my own life left me no example for Godly living, let alone being a model of real manhood;
- the testaments of men who came from a bloodline of thugs, gangsters, cheaters, liars, and crooks;
- how they explained that *their* fathers were not there for them;
- how the men in their families had "outside" children with different women;
- how men failed to be leaders in their homes and take care of their families.

Then I hear a whisper on the wind of a man who *was* there: a father who *did* stay; who *was* faithful; who *was* committed—yet went unrecognized and lived most of his adult life in the shadow of more dramatic stories of the men who abandoned their families—or worse. What kind of manly chaos is going on in his mind to be so courageous and strong, yet so taken for granted and overlooked? I realize that society is more interested in hearing (and repeating) sad, bad horror stories than happy, good uplifting stories, but at what cost?

Society may be psychologically programmed to expect bad news. For some reason, people like to be titillated and are drawn to negativity and drama. As a result, attention gets focused on the men who are *not* there. Our interest and our heads turn to the men who molest kids, leave their families, sleep with multiple women and take care of none. Just think about the headlines in the paper you picked up this morning or what gets reported on the TV—to say nothing of reality shows and music videos.

Our youth glory in music that is degrading to everyone and justify their preferences by saying, "That's how we talk to each other—so it's real, it's honest."

Really? Since when?

Since when did it become o.k. to call our daughters, girlfriends and wives "b****** and h**."

Since when?

We have to turn the corner *now*!

We must empower our men to live for God, for real. We must empower women to love their husbands with more than just their emotions. We have to empower sons and daughters to forgive their dads and give new meaning to their own lives in doing so.

Men need to be confronted in a new and different way by holding them accountable and celebrating them at the same time. I've been teaching young men who grew up without their fathers to do just that in a small group setting. They are learning to celebrate manhood *and* celebrate their fathers by recognizing the wonderful plan God had in bringing them into the world. They are learning to bypass the faults of their fathers and focus on the perfection of God, believing with all their hearts and minds that God has always had a plan for each of them and He called that plan into existence by who he choose to be their fathers. Together these young men are learning—and we should also learn—that celebration can't begin until the One who originated everything is acclaimed for what He has created through our fathers.

There are three components of this celebration we must bring together in order to truly begin applauding what it means to be a man. The first is acknowledging God's plan for our lives, because no man can celebrate manhood until he comes to the realization that he did not make himself a man. The second is celebrating our mothers, because no man could have done for himself what Momma's womb allowed to happen. The third is celebrating our men's lives, because we understand where they came from and who they came through and that's what makes them happy. That's what excites them. That's what makes them responsible. That's what's gives them perspective.

ATTITUDES AND ACTIONS

We started this book with A Man's Greatest Question: "Am I man enough?"

Men need to answer that question for themselves. And they need to answer that question now. Not just with words, but with meaningful daily action—the action of Power, Preparation and Purpose.

When men crucify their own ambitions and place those they care about in the center of their existence as the first and foremost reason to perform at their best, they change their lives and the lives of those around them. Obedience is always better than sacrifice. As a matter of fact, had it not been for the obedience of Jesus Christ, there would have been no sacrifice. It was His obedience that led Him to the cross. The same is true with men. Men who are obedient can really listen to God and do what He says. They can learn to make God-ordained sacrifices in their lives. They can learn to fall in love with the things that God wants for them. The desires of their hearts match the desires of God and they move on those things. In celebrating manhood, men need to fall in love with the responsibilities God has given them. Only when they hold on to their integrity and live in obedience to God can men celebrate their manhood, enjoying and accepting the tension that lies between leaving and staying when things get tough.

When men are prepared to face the inevitable adversities of life, they will find themselves rejoicing in the demise of the devil. They will live in the reality of "that which the devil meant for evil, God meant for good." A prepared man is a man who doesn't wait for a particular time or season to perform. A prepared man operates in every season of life and figures out how to maximize his efforts in that season.

When men find purpose, they change. They become focused and know exactly what it is that they are after. I tell men to look for results because, if you want to be able to celebrate yourself, you have to see what you are good at and observe what you are doing that is most effective. Men with purpose are alive and vibrant, not dead and confused. A man who has lived an unexamined life is a dead man. A man who is not aware of the things that drive him is a man who is in trouble. A man with purpose pays attention to the cues that may warn him that his attitudes and actions may be leading him to a sinful life and ultimately to his destruction. Instead, he engages in the things he has been purposed for. When men

16: Celebrating Manhood

celebrate manhood, they don't just focus on dreams, they focus on what they have and on what they are able to do and then they put all their God-given effort into that.

So celebrating manhood starts with each of us and it starts now. Begin thanking God for your father regardless of what he's done. Thank God for allowing you to be born. Thank Him for the man you have in your life. Remember, there may be someone out there who is praying for what you are taking for granted and the things you complain about.

And finally, to all the GREAT WOMEN who read this book, I say that I wish you the best and hope that this book has turned you to a deeper understanding of what makes a boy into a man, and to all the GREAT MEN they love, I hope you now turn toward true manhood in a much deeper way. I hope that I have set manhood under a magnifying glass and what you have seen helps you to live in celebration of it. I am closing this final chapter with a smile, hopeful that my words will have a positive impact on generations of men, women and children until the day Jesus returns to rapture us in victory and we shall meet our Heavenly Father.

> [5] *"Before I formed you in the womb I knew you,*
> *And before you were born I consecrated you;*
> *I have appointed you a prophet to the nations."*
> **(Jeremiah 1:5)**

Afterword

TO BOYS AND MEN

My hope is that life will make Godly men of you. I hope you honor and love the fact that God made you men. I hope you live as God-fearing men and, when your life has ended, you leave the mark of *Godly Manhood* behind.

Every man deserves the right to learn the hard lessons of life from another man. When he doesn't have that chance, there's a void so deep inside him that it makes it difficult for him to survive emotionally. But for you, I pray your fathers were there for you. If they were not, then I hope that your mothers were mature enough to know how much you needed that huge gap in your lives to be filled. I hope you find peace in the opportunity God now gives you to live as a man, to learn as a man and to lead as a man. I hope you never desire anything else but pure Godly Manhood.

So be a man, and be a *good* man. When being a man becomes tough—and it will—then be *more* of a man. Whatever you do in life, don't ever stop being—a man.

Amen.

> *And he shall turn the heart of the fathers to the children, and the heart of the children to their fathers...*
> **(Malachi 4:6 KJV)**

Index

A

abandoned children 143
abandoned families xix, 151
abandonment 48, 151
absentee fathers xiii, xx, xxi, 47, 123, 145, 147
absentee mothers 123
abuse, abusive xiii, 21, 34, 43, 143
    cycle of 76
abundance 137
accountability, accountable xv, xxv, xxvii, 34, 71, 104-105, 108, 134, 136, 152
achievement xxv
Act Like a Lady, Think Like a Man (Harvey) 10
Adam x, 26-27, 29, 120, 121-124, 129, 131, 138, 140
    world created for 29
adolescence 2
adversities (of life) 154
affirmation 5, 35-36, 48, 53, 77-78
aggression xxi, 53
aggressive 26, 53
altitude 77-78
    determined by attitude 78
American Sociological Review xxi
anger xxvii, 60-61, 67, 71, 74, 76-79, 84, 103, 116, 148
    as loss of control 76
    men's anger 77
    unresolved 61
    women's anger 76
appearance 7, 95
appreciation xi, 48, 53
assertive, assertiveness xxvii

B

basic components of crisis xxii
basic concepts of human development 49
basic necessities x, 49, 50
basics for helping sons build self-esteem 54
basics for men's survival 34
beginning, new 89,
behaviour xxi, xxii, 26, 52, 67, 76, 86, 95, 119-120, 124
    inappropriate 39
    disorders xx
    preventive vs. reactive 100-101
    risk-taking 26
belong, belonging 23, 34, 48, 53, 148
Bible references
    1 Corinthians 16:13 28
    Colossians 3:21 61
    Ecclesiastes 9:11 134
    Ephesians 6:4 60
    Ezekiel 22:30 6
    Galatians 3:26 69

Genesis 2:15 129
Genesis 2:21 26
Genesis 2:23 17
Genesis 3:19 124
Genesis 3:8-12 120
Hebrews 4:12 50
James 2:14 125
James 8:32 75
Jeremiah 1:5 155
John 1:3 41
Luke 1:31 62
Luke 6:38 140
Malachi 4:6 158
Mark 8:23 104
Matthew 6:33 94
Philippians 2:12 88
Proverbs 1:8-9 61
Proverbs 5:4 50
Proverbs 7:1-3 62
Proverbs 18:22 27
Proverbs 19:18 59
Proverbs 22:6 55, 59
Proverbs 24:16 111
Proverbs 31:28-29 45, 60
Psalm 1:1-6 20
Psalm 103:17 149
Psalm 119:9-16 38
Psalm 119:105 131
Psalm 149:6 50
Samuel 2:11 87
Timothy 1:7 79
"big circle" 89
boundaries 53, 123-124, 126, 136
boundary setting 53
boys x, xiv, xix, xx, xxi, xxvii, 2-5, 16, 22, 25-26, 29-32, 35-36, 39-41, 44, 47-52, 54-55, 57-58, 64-69, 71-72, 74, 86, 92, 95, 104, 108, 123, 129, 140-141, 145-147, 155, 157
boyhood 35, 63-65, 68
importance of father's presence 123
what boys need 40, 49, 54

C

calling men forward xvi
celebrate, celebration xi, 66, 68, 114, 152-155
three components of 153
Census Bureau (U.S. D.H.H.S.) xx
challenges, men's xii, 7, 21-24, 34, 44, 55, 65, 74, 77, 95, 116, 121,
change, changes ix, xxv-xxvi, xx, xxii-xxiii, xxviii, 9, 11-12, 24, 28, 43, 67-68, 73, 84, 88, 94, 96, 104, 108, 110-111, 140, 142, 144, 154
a woman's prerogative 115
accepting change 110
direction 130
of heart 88
character xi, xviii, xxvi-xxvii, 26, 60, 65, 77, 81-82, 86
Charles F. Kettering Foundation xxii
cheaters, cheating xxvii, 37, 88, 90, 100-101, 103, 151
child-parent bond 144
choice, choices xv, xxv-xxvi, 109-110, 127
Christ 3, 22, 24, 67, 69, 138, 148, 154
as Savior 148
Christian 11, 64, 78, 92, 106, 132, 136, 138, 166
Church, the xxiv, 2-3, 11, 34, 48, 57, 84-85, 117, 133, 148
"circle in the circle" 83
commerce 117, 119 see also: marketing
commitment xii, 13, 16, 57, 59, 71, 81-84, 106, 123-124
See also: Four Commitments, the
communication 12, 115,
communication skills 115, 121
conflict xxii-xxiv, 61, 142
confusion xxii, xxiv, 23

control, controlling xxvii, 10, 16, 20, 25, 39-40, 43, 68, 75-77, 116, 123, 129, 135
conversation, value of 12
Corey's Story 51
Creator, the 30, 121
crisis (of manhood) xiv, xvii, xxi-xxiii, xxiv, xxvii
   defined xx
   dynamic of xxii, xxiv
   effects of xxvii
   four basic components xxii
   research xx-xxii
   role of the Church 3
   world problem xx

D

danger, dangerous 5, 14, 76, 95, 138
   see also: behaviour, risk-taking
deadbeat dads xiv
dead ends 94, 127-131
decision xxii, xxvi, xxvii, 3, 13-14, 21, 78, 85-86, 97, 104, 119, 130-131, 134, 137
Desire Street Ministries 136
desire, desired ix, xi, xii, xxiv, xxv, xxvii, 8, 11, 14-16, 31, 37, 45, 49, 92, 110, 136, 139, 154
destiny xxiii, 97, 119, 138
devil, the 63, 78, 138, 154,
Diary of a Mad Black Woman (Perry) 76
discipline 40, 48-50, 53, 60, 64-65, 79, 81-82, 88
divorce xxii, 48, 58
domestic violence 76
door of opportunity 90-941
double-edged sword 50-52, 54, 72
dreams, chasing 128, 136
drugs, drug dealers xiv, 4, 21, 93, 117, 129, 144

E

economics xxviii, 23
Einstein, Albert 111
emotional balance xxvii
emotional detachment 33, 48, 89
emotional energy 4
emotional support ix, xxiii, 21, 25-26, 53, 55, 140, 147
emotions 8-9, 14, 21, 35, 44, 48, 52, 55, 60, 76-77, 83, 97, 106, 110, 115-116, 118-119, 122-123, 138, 140, 154
   men's emotions 44, 76-77, 110, 115-116, 138, 157
empowerment xv, xxvi, 61, 93, 95, 146-147, 152, 154
exploration, explore xvii, 15, 40, 80, 116

F

fail, failure, failing xix, xxv, 13, 47, 72, 88-89, 93, 105-110, 113, 118, 132-134, 138, 148, 151
faith 24, 28, 65, 69, 99, 101, 121, 123, 125, 133, 135, 148-149
faithful xv
faithfulness 87-88, 93, 151
family xiii, xv, xix, xxi, xxiii, xxv, 2, 10, 12, 24, 28-29, 53, 58-59, 61, 71, 74, 76, 83-85, 92, 99, 103, 106 117-119, 136, 142-143, 148-149
father, fathers ix-x, xiv, xvi, xx-xxii, 4-5, 22, 35, 40, 43-44, 47-48, 50-68, 99, 102, 107, 109, 117, 125-, 141, 143, 146-150, 153-154, 157
   daddy 64
   imprisoned xi, 4-5, 144
Father Absence and Youth Incarceration (Journal of Research on Adolescence) xx

father figure 134
fatherless xx, xxi, 2, 58, 73, 152
   see also: absentee fathers
Fatherless Children (Adams, Milner & Schrepf) xxi
fathers and mothers xiv, xxii, 53-54, 64, 143
   role of 47
fear, fears xxiv-xxv, xxvii, 24, 34, 61, 71, 74-75, 88-89, 96, 100, 105-106, 116, 121-124
   expressed as anger 74
   "healthy" fear 75
   objective of 75
   overcoming 74-75
fearful 34, 74, 79, 144
fearless 24
feel, feelings x-xviii, xxvii, 1, 3-5, 7-9, 13-15, 20, 22-23, 25-28, 30, 32, 34-37, 39, 43-44, 51-52, 60-61, 66-67, 75-78, 83-84, 87, 89, 96-98, 105, 107-108, 113-120, 122-123, 125, 128, 130-131, 138-139, 140, 142, 145
filter 100, 115, 124, 125
   filtering laboratory 125
   filtering process 122
finances, financial support 21
flexibility, flexible 130-131
focus xi-xii, xix, 3, 15, 26-27, 33, 49, 52-54, 78, 90, 101-102, 109, 127-128, 131-132, 137, 143, 145, 130, 137, 143, 145, 147-148, 151, 153-155
Four Commitments, the 82, 84
Franklin, Benjamin 111
funnel living 135, 137-138, 140

G

gay 3
gender identity, gender roles 12, 50
genitals 39
glass ceiling 78

goals xi, 29-30, 78, 87, 106, 118, 127-128
   pursuing vs chasing dreams 128
God and family 59
God as "good parent" 59
God, obedience to 154
God, Kingdom of 41-42, 148
God, surrender to 98
God's call to man xii, 23, 32, 34-35, 41, 43-44, 55, 64-65, 76, 84, 105, 133-134, 153
God's concern for children 61
God's intent for men xv
God's objective, plan 21, 61-62, 152
God's will 134
God's word 24, 50, 131-132
God-fearing 157
Godly development 61
Godly instruction 61
Godly living 90, 151
Godly man, manhood, men ix, 3, 20, 23, 76, 107, 141, 157
   definition of ix
gratification, instant 117, 132
greatness, opportunity for 27
growing up 61-62
   from inside out 62
guilt xxiii, 13, 15, 32, 35, 51, 101, 103, 118-119
guilty conscience 118

H

Harvey, Steve 10
healthy choices 127
healthy family xiv, 48, 142
healthy food 21
healthy life, lifestyle 129
healthy mind 27
healthy relationships ix, 43
healthy sexuality 15
healthy sons ix, 48, 50
heterosexual 3
home
   single-parent xxi-xxii, xvi, 50, 136

two-parent xxi, 51
homosexuality *see* gay
honest, honesty xviii, xxvii, 11-13, 86, 97, 100-103, 108-109, 120, 152
hitting bottom 88, 108
"Household Family Structure and Children's Aggressive Behavior" (Vaden-Kieman, et al.) xxi
Hurricane Katrina 135
husband and wife, as equal partners xv

I

imprison, imprisoned xi
indiscretion, owning up to 101
inflexible 128
instant gratification 117, 132
integrity xxv, xxviii, 26, 85-88, 90, 101, 153
   defined 86
intimate, intimacy x 10, 13, 15, 21, 86, 106, 123

J

jail xx, 5, 71 *see also:* prison, imprison
jealousy xxiv
Jeffrey's Story 101
Joe's Story xvii
Journal of Abnormal Child Psychology xxi
Journal of Research on Adolescence xx
Joyce's Story 146
judging, judgment 5, 20, 22, 24, 45, 50
Justice, U.S. Dept. of xxi
juvenile(s) xxii
juvenile delinquents xxii

K

keys 41, 43, 90-94
and doors 43, 90-94
keys to the city 91
Kingdom of God 41-42, 148
Kingdom of Heaven 41
Kingdom Priorities 142, 148-149
   definition of 142
   principles of 142-147

L

leap of faith 133
Leverett, Mo 135
location 133-134
   and vision 134
locomotion 82, 113, 121-122, 124-125
logic, logical 9-10, 48, 52, 82, 84, 86-87, 113, 115-116, 119, 120-122, 124-125, 135
love ix, x-xii, xv, xx, xxiv-xxvi, 8-9, 15, 21, 24-25, 34-37, 40, 44, 48-54, 57
   difficult for men 12
Love Notes (Scott) 97

M

Madison Avenue 27
man *see:* manhood, men, real man/men
man enough xviii, 1, 20-21, 155
man up xii, xvi, xix, 78
man words 54
manhood xviii, xix, xxi-xxii, xxiv-xxviii, 2-5, 7, 19, 20, 23, 25, 27-28. 40-41, 43-44, 57, 63-65, 68-69, 71, 76, 82, 95, 98, 116-117, 129, 137, 139, 151-155, 157
   and Madison Avenue 27
   character, characteristics of manhood xxvi-xxvii
   definition of xxvii
   healthy manhood 63, 65, 83
   in the Church, issue of 3
   manhood crisis xvii, xxii, xix, xxiv

measure of 2, 19-20, 22, 25, 28
threat to 43
see also: Godly manhood, University of Manhood
manly xxiii, xxiv-xxvii, 2, 21, 26, 74, 139, 153 see also: real men
marketing xix, 27-28, 142 see also: commerce
measure of success 145
measure up 2
Mental Interpretation (of events) 99
Marmion (Scott) 101
marriage xv, xvii-xviii, 12, 87, 98, 101, 103, 117-118
 challenges in 12
 and restoring manhood 117
masculine, masculinity xix, 19, 22, 77, 139
 two-fold (inside and outside) 22
media x, xix, xxv, 2
mediate, mediator 141-143, 146-147
men
 abusive xiii, 34, 43, 76
 and loyalty xi-xii
 and sex xiii, 87
 and strength 94
 as leaders xxv, 25, 64, 98, 117, 149, 151
 as examples/role models 2, 148, 151
 challenges for xii, 7, 21-24, 34, 44, 55, 65, 74, 77, 95, 116, 121
 how men think 7-8
 insight into ix, xiii, xvi, 48, 64
 interior voices 23
 love of power xxvii, 20, 130
 made for production 131
 men's biggest question 1
 outside influences x, xix
 real (man, men) 16, 21, 32, 104, 109, 117, 148, 151
 role in society xxiv-xxv

shortcomings of 15
 what men need xi-xii, 34, 36, 49
 what men want xi, 34, 120, 139
 what women think about 9
mentoring, mentors xvii, 2, 4, 65, 72, 105, 108, 142, 145-147, 141
 as rescuers 145-146
mentorship programs 145
 challenging the concept 141
message to men (author's) 78
mother ix-x, xiv-xv, xvii, xxi-xxii, 5, 30, 32-33, 36, 39-44, 50-55, 7-58, 60-61, 63-64, 68, 72, 90, 92-93, 114-115, 123, 143-149. 153, 157
 mama's boy 58, 63, 65
 Momma 22, 31, 42-44, 58, 63, 65, 72, 153
mother and father see: father and mother
mother-only households xxi see also: homes, single-parent
mom and dad, role of 57
motivate, motivation, motivational xvi, 23, 67, 81, 83, 1-3. 129, 139
music 2, 141, 152

N

National Institute of Justice xx
National Principals Association xxi
Networking 131
new beginning 89
non-aggressive 117

O

obedience to God 154
objective(s)
 author's xiv, xv, 5
 of families 142
 of God 33

of life 29, 142
of women 33, 55
of fear 75
Office for Weed and Seed xx
One-Parent Families and Their Children (Charles F. Kettering Foundation) xxii
opportunity
  doors of 90-91, 93-94
  financial 26
  for change xxii, xxv-xxvi
  for commitment to self 83
  for focus 15
  for greatness 27
  for restoration 68
  for self-observation 14
  for sons to talk about their fathers 66
  God-given 92, 157
  management 29
  maximizing 91-92
  missed 130
  new 90-91
  taking advantage of 92
  to be a son 65
  to correct problems (parents) 143
  to be vulnerable 32
  to forgive 67
  to impact people 92
  to life 84
  to show fear 74
  to understand relationships 61

P

paradigm, paradigm shift xxiii, 19, 43, 48, 64, 142
parent, parenting x, xii-xiii, xix-xxii, 25, 33, 47-51, 54, 59, 72, 94, 117, 143-148
  child-parent bond 144
  not a concrete science 48
  single- xxii, 136
  see also: homes, single- and two-parent

partners 15, 62, 88, 94, 96, 106, 110, 119
  husband and wife as equal xv
paying it forward 135
Perry, Tyler 76
personal gain, temptation of 138
phallus, as work of Creator 39
physical risk 26 *see also:* risk-taking
potential x, xiii, 78, 82, 91, 114
poverty 45, 92, 136
power xxiv, 20, 25, 28, 40, 65, 75, 78-79, 81, 85, 91, 129-130
  and anger 76
  loss of xxiv
  of evil 64
  of fear 75
  of groups 84
  of love 98, 101
  of marriage 117
  of perspective 95
  of rituals 15
  of women x, 41, 43
Power, Preparation and Purpose 153
powerless 76, 117
pride 138, 109
prison 4, 68, 144
projects 36, 129
projection 4, 15
promises 115
purpose 7, 23-25, 29, 31, 47, 49, 106, 115, 142, 147, 153-154
pushing and calling 55, 64
  pushed and called 32, 43

Q-R

real man/ men 16, 21, 32, 104, 109, 117, 148, 151,
redemption 97, 122, 124, 141-142, 145-146
redemptive mediation 147
Redemptive Son-ship 58, 63-66
  see also: son-ship

redemptive worker 145-146
reflection 59-60, 64, 66, 75, 107,
relationship(s) ix-xiiv, xvii-xviii, xxv, xxvii, 12-16, 22-25, 30-40, 42-43, 51-52, 57-19, 61, 63, 56, 71, 83, 86, 88, 90, 94, 97-98, 101-103, 106, 119-120, 123, 138-139, 141, 146, 147-149
   essentials of 115
   with/to God xxv, 17
research xiv, xx-xxi, xxv, 47-48
   achievement xxi
   agression xxi
   behavioral disorders xx
   confused identities xxi
   criminal activity xxii
   delinquency xxii
   educational attainment xxi
   high school dropouts xxi
   incarceration rates xx
   juvenile detention rates xxi
   suicide xx
resiliency, resilient 95, 144
resolution xxvii, 67
resolve 23, 30, 33, 42, 67, 95, 108, 116, 142-146
respect, respected, respectful, respecting x-xi, xxvii, 11, 16, 21, 28, 34-35, 41, 49, 54, 59, 65, 75, 84, 87-88
responsible, responsibility ix, xi, xv, xxii-xxiii, xxiv-xxv, xxvii, xix, 4, 7, 13-14, 23-24, 27, 33-34, 40, 52-53, 58 -59, 71, 77, 79, 81, 83-85, 95-98, 100-101, 105-106, 108, 116-117, 124, 131-132, 134, 136, 143, 153-154
restoration, restore xxv, 5, 63, 68, 117, 124-145
rituals, power of 15
role of mom and dad 47

S

safe, safety xviii, 31-32, 34, 41, 43-44, 49, 54, 74, 96, 116, 122, 129
Scott, Sir Walter 101
scripture 34, 41, 59, 61-62, 121, 138 *see also:* Bible references
seduce, seduction 13, 87
self-actualization 69, 82
self-awareness 26
self-esteem 49, 54, 61, 77, 147
self-evaluation 25-26
self-examination xxvi, 26
self-exploration 82
self-identity 147
self-image 26, 49, 54
self-realization 82
self-reflection xxvii
self-reproach 119
self-satisfaction 3
self-worth 25, 49
selfishness 138
selflessness 37
sex x, xii, 4, 9-116, 28, 33, 37, 39, 42-44, 82, 102, 110, 117, 125, 144
   illicit xvi
   indiscriminate 43
   postponing 13-14
   symbols 27
sexual beings, men as xiii
sexual conquest 15
sexual development 116
sexual experience 148
sexual immorality 3
sexual misconduct 87
sexual neediness, in men xx
sexual relationships 42
sexual roles xxi, 12
sexual stimulation 39
sexual struggles 32, 39
sexual temptation 40, 87
sexuality xii-xiii, xxiv, 15, 32, 29, 55
sexy 27-28, 118
shalom 143

shame 35, 76, 103, 105, 123-124
shortcomings 15
   isolation 15, 123
   lack of consistency 15
   lack of trust 15
sense of sexual conquest 15
single-parent home *see:* home
six keys 94
society, feminine nature of 117
soft stuff 139-142
son-ship 4-5, 40-41, 44, 58, 61, 63-69
   as training ground for real life 65
   stages of 66
   see also: Redemptive Son-ship
sowing and reaping 32
sowing seeds 141
Spencer's Story 143
spouse 86, 101
status 23, 25
status quo 111
stepfamilies xxi
strength xxviii, 20, 22, 45, 93, 95, 98-99, 109, 114
subordination 61
success 23, 89, 130
   measure of 145
survival, survive xviii, 32, 34, 141, 146, 157

T

temptation xxv, 14, 40, 87, 121, 138
truth xiv, xix, xxvi, 3, 10-13, 20, 27, 58, 60, 68, 73-74, 76-77, 86, 100-101, 103-104
   as prerequisite to trust 103
trust 15, 54, 96, 103, 113, 135
   lack of 15

U

unaccountable 124

Unbreaking the Heart (Scott) xii, 99
Underclass Behaviours in the United States (Hill & O'Neill) xxii
unexamined life 154
unresolved anger 61
U.S. Dept. of Justice xxi

V

victim(s) xiv, 75-78
victim mentality 77
vision 130, 132-133

W

What Can the Federal Government Do to Decrease Crime and Revitalize Communities? (U.S. D.H.H.S., Bureau of Census) xx
what men want xi, 34, 120, 139
   soft stuff 139
what parents should say to their sons 54
what women think about men 9
wife, wives ix, xiii, xvii, xix, xxiv, 3, 13, 15, 24-25, 27, 33, 34 43-44, 67-68, 85, 93, 96-98, 100-103, 113, 120, 129, 138, 140, 149, 152, 165
   as friend 44
Wilbert's Story 106
Wisconsin Dept. of Health and Social Services xxii
womb 29, 30-32, 40-45, 55, 62, 153, 155
woman, women ix-xvi, xix-xx, xxiii-xxiv, xxvi-xxvii, 1, 5, 7, 9-17, 21, 23, 27-28, 30, 32-33, 35, 38, 40, 42-45, 47, 50, 55, 60, 65, 74, 76, 81-82, 87, 90, 95-96, 102-103, 106, 109-110, 113, 125, 127, 133, 139, 148-149
   and anger 76

as sex symbols 27-28
filling men's shoes xxiii
how women think 9, 13, 119
"liberated" 43
sexual desire of 10-11, 13-14
what women want 10
world of 74
word(s) xii, xvii, xix, 24-25, 35, 38, 50, 52, 54, 59, 62, 75, 81, 85, 91, 96, 111, 113-114, 131-132,
as bond 114
misinterpretation of 114,
of God 24, 50, 131-132
work, worked, working xv, xviii, xxii, xxvi, 1, 8, 24, 33, 36, 71, 78, 83-84, 88, 90, 93, 102, 109, 128-129, 130-131, 137-139, 142, 149
world, as a management opportunity 29

X-Y-Z

About the Author

Leroy Scott is an author and Christian Counselor. His extensive experience working with men, women, couples and families spans more than 18 years. He holds a Master's degree in counseling and psychology and a Master of Divinity degree. Over the past 10 years, he has become one of America's leading authorities on building healthy relationships. When he is not traveling around the country to workshops, seminars and speaking engagements, Scott lives in Louisiana with his wife and three children – who are the reason for everything he does.

CONTACT INFORMATION

Leroy Scott Ministries
5635 Main Street
Suite A / #184
Zachary, LA 70791

http://leroyscott.com/contact-leroy-scott/

OTHER PRODUCTS

Creating Possibilities in Marriage
ISBN: 978-1-61579-436-2
Copyright: 2009
Price: $9.99

Love Notes:
28 Ways to Deepen Your Love Life
ISBN: 978-0-615-78278-2
Copyright: 2013
Price: $23.99

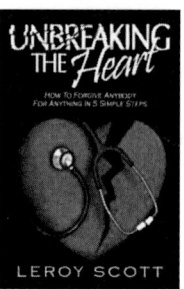

Unbreaking the Heart
How to Forgive Anybody for Anything in 5 Simple Steps
ISBN: 978-0-578-08523-4
Price: $19.99

To order visit: www.leroyscott.com